Fundamentals of Selling

The Sales Track

JIM NORRED

Outskirts Press, Inc.
Denver, Colorado

The opinions expressed in this manuscript are solely the opinions of the author and do not represent the opinions or thoughts of the publisher. The author has represented and warranted full ownership and/or legal right to publish all the materials in this book.

Fundamentals of Selling
The Sales Track
All Rights Reserved.
Copyright © 2011 Jim Norred
V3.0

This book may not be reproduced, transmitted, or stored in whole or in part by any means, including graphic, electronic, or mechanical without the express written consent of the publisher except in the case of brief quotations embodied in critical articles and reviews.

Outskirts Press, Inc.
http://www.outskirtspress.com

ISBN: 978-1-4327-6068-7

Outskirts Press and the "OP" logo are trademarks belonging to Outskirts Press, Inc.

PRINTED IN THE UNITED STATES OF AMERICA

"Selling is knowing what to say, how to say it, and when to say it."

Jim Norred

In Memoriam

This book is dedicated to the loving memory of Patrick L. Collins, an excellent sales manager, my mentor, a great friend, and an all around nice guy.

Table of Contents

Introduction ix
Chapter 1 1
   The *"Professional"* Salesperson
Chapter 2 9
   The "Sales Track" Concept
Chapter 3 19
   The Approach: You Can't Sell 'Em if
     They Won't Let You Tell 'Em!
- The critical importance of opening statements
- The prospect/customer's perspective
- How Creative Thinking Broke Down the Barrier
- The Added Impact of a Visual Piece
- The Best Sales Comeback Ever – The *"Stun Statement"*
- The Telephone Approach
- The "Gatekeeper"

Chapter 4 55
   Effective Diagnosing
- Uncovering buying motives
- "Open-ended" verses "Closed-ended" questions

Chapter 5 67

Presenting With Benefits Builds Desire &
Creates Conviction
- Features versus Benefits
- Building conviction

Chapter 6 91
Objections: Obstacles or Opportunities?
- Objections handling formula
- "Blitzing" - How to sack a recurring tough objection
- Hostile Encounters & "Disarming" Techniques

Chapter 7 119
Closing the Sale
- The psychology of closing
- Types of closes
- Nullifying the dreaded "I'd like to think it over" stall
- Effective call back strategies

Chapter 8 147
Game Winning Plays

Chapter 9 181
Staying on Track

Epilogue 189
Onward the Quest!

Sales Call Evaluation Form 191
Index 195
About the Author 199

Introduction

Congratulations on investing in your success. It is my utmost desire to ensure that you conclude that this purchase proved to be a worthwhile investment. When I decided to write this book, I knew that I wanted something unique from the numerous other inspirational sales books that have been written over the years. Please don't get me wrong. Such books from respected authors like Zig Ziglar, Tom Hopkins, Percy Whiting, and many others have inspired millions of readers, me included. I merely wanted more of a concise nuts-and-bolts framework that could serve as a blueprint for building effective sales presentations and designing selling strategies.

Think of this as a textbook on the fundamentals of selling and effective sales strategies. Basic selling skills and techniques haven't changed that much over the years. They transcend our technology-driven lifestyles. Although eLearning solutions and web conferencing have certainly enhanced the training capabilities of corporate sales training departments, such technologies are delivery systems only that still require meaningful effective content. At its most elementary level, selling is simply knowing ***what to say, how to say it, and when to say it.***

What can you expect to get out of this book? Like most endeavors, it depends on how much time, effort, and concentration you put into studying these concepts. Bear in mind that this is a training course and, as such, demands your utmost focus and attention. There may be topics you'll need to reread two or three times to fully grasp. I've tried to keep the reading interesting and enjoyable with the use of anecdotes and analogies to make and illustrate points. I also intentionally designed this manual with "Notes" pages and "Skills Development Exercises" so that you can develop it into your own personal sales textbook. If a particular paragraph triggers an idea for your sales situation or training program, jot it down immediately because ideas can be very fleeting. In doing so, this manual becomes a collaborative effort to design a custom sales plan that's unique to your precise selling needs.

I've tried to convey a sense of the challenges that sales people face daily and how mastering these fundamental selling skills can provide the confidence needed to overcome them. As with any endeavor, when you begin to gain confidence in your abilities and skill level, it becomes much more enjoyable. Then, instead of experiencing apprehension or anxiety over how you'll perform, it becomes fun and exciting.

I truly believe that if you devote adequate time and effort to reading this book and participating in the skills development exercises, you'll be rewarded with a solid understanding and foundation of fundamental selling skills. If you're an experienced salesperson already, then this should be a great refresher course for you. For sales trainers and managers, this book provides an excellent framework to build a basic sales training program around.

Selling can be a very noble and gratifying profession. It can provide a lucrative livelihood for you and your family. But like all vocations, it requires a personal commitment to excellence if you want to be above average. If you perceive sales to be an occupation where manipulative skills and arrogance are pluses, then your success will be short lived. If, on the other hand, you view it as an opportunity to help people find solutions to problems and realize their dreams, then you have the potential to do well in this profession. Zig Ziglar put it well when he said, "You can have everything in life you want if you will just help enough other people get what they want."

As you progress through the chapters in this book, you'll notice that I occasionally describe it as a workbook, so allow me to explain why. It's simply because I intentionally structured this sales training manual to engage the reader in designing sales strategies suitable for them. As a sales trainer, I've always been inclined to try to analyze the cause and effect of sales interactions. By understanding the buyer/prospect's perspective, I believe that you can better formulate effective sales strategies.

I hope you will be inclined to participate in devising solutions to the challenges you face everyday in your sales position. I honestly believe that if you apply the concepts I present in this manual, then you can achieve this very effectively. If you are new to sales or simply aspire to this profession, make this a participatory exercise whereby you aren't just a reader but a problem solver and architect for your own success.

As for me personally, my path into sales was more coincidence than by design. After graduating from college, my ambitions were to be a marketing research rep for a Fortune 500 company such as Proctor & Gamble, General Electric, or Johnson & Johnson. I aligned myself with an Atlanta-based recruiting firm that specialized in placing ex-military officers. They succeeded in arranging interviews for me with some of my target companies; however, the entry-level territory manager positions were a bit disappointing to me. All of them offered a starting salary that was considerably less than what I had been making as an Army captain. Also, I had to be willing to relocate anywhere in the U.S. upon completion of the company's initial training.

It was then that I decided to explore the sales profession, and I soon landed an outside sales position with a major Yellow Pages advertising firm located in Tampa, Florida. This was an excellent introduction into outside sales because of the broad diversity of business types available for me to sell to. Also, the sales cycle was relatively brief and therefore, required excellent selling skills in order to achieve quick results and meet the company's expectations.

Fortunately, this particular company had a very thorough initial sales training program, plus, my first sales manager proved to be a great teacher and mentor. After a year and a half as a sales representative, I was promoted to regional sales trainer and, thus, began my pursuit of sales training excellence. Since then, I have administered sales training programs and developed training manuals for Yellow Pages companies, the interconnect telephone equipment industry, electric utilities, and others.

I certainly don't claim to have conceived all the ideas and concepts presented in this manual. I've thoroughly studied the intricacies of selling through noted sales trainers that I mentioned earlier: Zig Ziglar, Tom Hopkins, Percy H. Whiting, J. Douglas Edwards, Brian Tracy, and others. Most of their teachings ultimately sparked ideas of my own where I've tweaked concepts to suit my particular selling situation at the time.

I've also been fortunate to have been associated with some superb salespeople and sales managers over the years. What I learned from them was to take a good idea and mold it to your own style and set of circumstances. Then you own it and can more effectively internalize it.

Although I recount some stories from my Yellow Pages days, please don't conclude that this book was designed to be a sales manual especially for that industry. I've done so in the hope of stimulating your thinking and to spark some ideas for your particular selling situation. These sales concepts are transferrable to virtually any type product or service. Creative thinking has always been a hallmark of good salespeople, and that shall forever be the case.

For the benefit of those readers who aspire to sales and want to better understand what some of the expectations of prospective employers might be, I offer these observations. Some of the early interviews I had with Fortune 500 companies in Atlanta were for territory sales positions. I, perhaps like you, had little or no introduction to professional selling skills in my previous jobs. Nonetheless, I occasionally encountered the old "sell me this stapler or ball point pen" scenario from my interviewer. Needless to say, my expert marksmanship with an M-16 rifle or my military leadership training hadn't adequately prepared me for this test of sales prowess.

I guess these interviewers wanted to see how tenacious I could be in out arguing them over whether they should buy their own pen. Regrettably, these interviews didn't go particularly well, and I almost decided that sales might not be the best vocational choice for me after all. Then when a personnel agency in Tampa managed to secure me an interview with a Yellow Pages firm even though they knew I had no prior sales experience, I decided to go with a more relaxed, nothing-to-lose attitude. I further decided that if they hit me with the old "sell me this pen" exercise, I would respond by saying that my military experience had taught me that it's best to master fundamental skills before you try to demonstrate them.

For example, I was not allowed to fire an M-60 automatic weapon until I had gone through several hours of classroom instruction. My point, I continued, was that tenacity in the absence of effective selling skills is nothing more than verbal pugilism.

I stressed that my background of successfully achieving excellence in my academic and occupational endeavors should translate into similar success in sales given adequate training. My strategy resulted in me receiving a job offer from this company. As a seasoned sales training professional now, I truly hope this ridiculous interviewing tactic is no longer practiced, at least by reputable companies. In my opinion, the only thing it shows is a lack of imagination on the part of the interviewer.

There are sales aptitude tests that have proven to be excellent predictors of a candidate's viability for a sales position. If an interviewer truly wants to gauge how well a person thinks on his or her feet during an interview, they should ask that person a question like, "How would you go about convincing your colleagues to support your position or recommendations?"

If you still fall victim to the "sell me this pen" interview tactic, I suggest you employ my strategy and say something like, "I have to assume that this is a trick question since I doubt that verbal combative skills have much relevance to the professional selling techniques I would expect your company training would provide me with." Just remember that it takes much more skill and finesse to lead a prospect into making a buying decision that they feel good about than it does to simply verbally pummel them into submission.

The main reason for me sharing my personal story of how I got into sales is to support my contention that good salespeople aren't born, they're made. Certainly there are some characteristic traits that are favorable to selling such as good conversational skills and being an extrovert rather than an introvert. That being said, the real opportunity for success in sales lies within each individual and his or her personal desire to succeed. The methods I present in this training manual can help sales aspirants understand the underlying psychology of the sales process and better prepare them to effectively interview with prospective employers.

Equally important, this manual offers numerous ideas and recommendations for sales novices, seasoned veterans, and sales managers or trainers looking to reinforce their existing skills or add some creative ideas to their sales training. It simply boils down to how much effort you're willing to devote in making the most that this manual can deliver. I promise that if you'll put forth the effort and follow the recommendations outlined herein, you'll see noticeable improvement in your sales effectiveness and results. Now, like the recent U.S. Army recruiting ad said, "Be All That You Can Be!" Choose to be a winner and *Go For It!*

Chapter 1

The *"Professional"* Salesperson

Most recipients of this workbook are either in sales or they aspire to the profession of sales. Note that the word "profession" is the base word for the term "professional." Oftentimes, people reserve the designation "Pro" for sports figures or for those individuals who, by virtue of their education, are in highly paid occupations such as doctors, attorneys, or engineers.

The dictionary defines "professional" as "Having great skill in a particular field or activity." Therefore, such a distinction is not exclusive to certain vocations only. And yet, it's still not uncommon for people to perceive their family doctor or lawyer as being on a higher level of esteem than they consider attainable for themselves in their chosen field.

Your attitude about yourself has tremendous influence on your performance level and potential for success. It is a self-fulfilling prophecy. As you conceive of yourself, so shall it be. The truth, then, is that the real opportunity for success lies within the person and not the position.

Professionalism, although a self-endowed trait, still requires ongoing maintenance on your part. If you ever change jobs due to a better opportunity, your standard of professional conduct and your skill level will help ensure your continued success in your new career.

Success in selling, as with any endeavor, does not occur haphazardly. It must be a well planned and executed strategy. The potential rewards in selling, in terms of both financial and emotional compensation, can be astronomical. Such rewards, however, are directly proportionate to the demands made upon your selling skills and attitude.

As an example, the counter clerk at a McDonald's restaurant is, technically speaking, a salesperson. They even incorporate some selling into their job by being trained to always ask if you want to upsize your order or if you'd like an apple pie with your meal.

But I bet you'll never witness a counter clerk walk over to their manager having just served a customer and say something like, "Wow, I just sold this guy three Big Mac's, four large fries, and two large drinks, and all he originally wanted was a cheeseburger!" The reason is simple. The incentive to encourage such ambitious selling at McDonald's does not exist because the demands on selling skills are minimal. The big bucks in sales are not found in those jobs where customers are willing to stand in line to give someone their order.

To illustrate another point, consider some of the highly successful multilevel marketing organizations such as Amway. Their introductory recruiting sessions are fantastic at injecting excitement and enthusiasm into their audiences. Thousands of new associates are recruited every week into Amway at such rallies. And yet, the fact is that less than five percent of those individuals who join such ventures ever achieve a high level of financial success.

My intent here is not to belittle the opportunity, but rather to suggest that enthusiasm is quickly diluted by a scarcity of successes due to inadequate selling skills. Enthusiasm is merely fuel for the vehicle. It is not the vehicle. The correlation to these two points is that the potential for high compensation will typically be found in those fields where salespeople must possess the ability to *persuade* prospects to take favorable action on their proposals.

Much of the sales training being offered today focuses heavily on motivational concepts and generalized selling philosophies. They also devote a great deal of discussion on peripheral issues such as how to sustain sales momentum, solicit referrals, customer retention, contact management systems, and time management. These are all important enhancements to a solid foundation of selling fundamentals.

In this workbook, I chose to concentrate strictly on the substance of professional selling skills and how they relate to the sales process. The objective of this workbook is to arm you with proven sales techniques that will allow you to effectively engage prospects and close them on

The *"Professional"* Salesperson

your recommendations.

This *Sales Track* sales manual is essentially like military basic training (hence "SalesCadre[1].com") that focuses solely on teaching you the fundamental skills of professional selling. It will, however, require an effort on your part to internalize these techniques so that YOU own them.

Selling does not typically thrive in an improvisational manner. It must be a well conceived and executed strategy borne of thorough preparation. The ability of a skilled salesperson to respond effectively to prospect resistance and objections occurs best when it's attributed to well devised and carefully formulated responses.

Most people have an innate resistance to being sold. However, just about everyone loves to buy. Your role as a professional salesperson is to help facilitate this process. Thorough preparation enhances execution in any skill. This is especially true in professional selling. You

---

[1] "Cadre" is defined as a group of trained or otherwise qualified personnel capable of forming, training, or leading an organization.

must ensure that all facets of your game are well polished if you are to succeed on a high level in sales today.

Sales also affords you the opportunity to control your own destiny, probably more than any other profession. By your willingness to work harder, longer, be more creative, determined, disciplined, resourceful, and simply desiring to achieve excellence and be successful, you can make it happen for yourself. Does this require hard work and an intense desire to be the best? The answer, of course, is yes. Just remember this axiom if you ever question if it's worth the effort:

EXHILARATION RARELY COMES FROM DOING THINGS THAT ARE EASY!

Let the journey begin!

The Sales Track

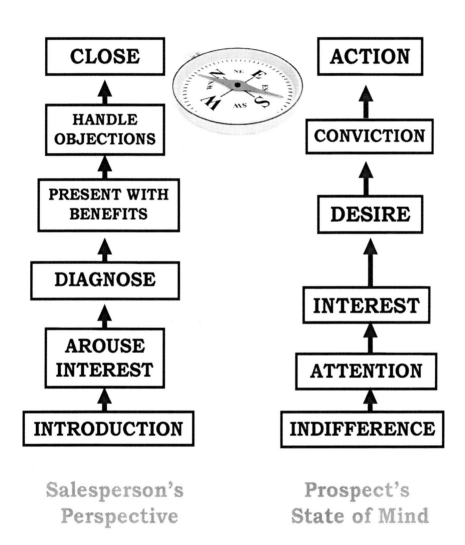

Chapter 2

The "Sales Track" Concept

Trying to diagram the sales process would be comparable to trying to graphically depict how life should play out. It's just too dynamic to accurately portray. Therefore, what I've tried to do here is to illustrate a sales track that, all things being perfect, would be the typical course of a sales presentation in an ideal environment. Understanding this, you also need to recognize that selling does not always lend itself to a predictable course. From the very onset, your introduction can be cut short by a hostile or unreceptive prospect. Whether deserved or not, this can shut down your sales presentation before it even gets off the ground.

View this Sales Track as a blueprint of how a sales presentation *should ideally go*. This graphic simply provides you with a track to follow. You should ultimately design your default presentation to conform to this structure, allowing for the variables you could potentially encounter. It's important to understand that effective salespeople must become adept at being versatile and innovative when things don't always occur in a logical sequence. The critical element here is how effectively you are able to quickly respond to variations in this strategy.

Selling is definitely *not* simply delivering a well rehearsed speech. It is a constantly changing scenario that demands flexibility and resilience on your part. The actual act of selling could generally be described as engaging a prospect or customer in a sales dialogue with the intent of persuading them to act favorably on your proposal. The time frame for closing them on your proposal varies from immediately to sometimes months, depending on the product or service you're selling. Door-to-door security systems salespeople attempt to close on the spot. A person selling corporate jets would more likely expect a sales cycle that could encompass many months before the deal is finalized.

The "Sales Track" Concept

Of course, the following old adage always applies in sales. When is the best time to close? That would be ***whenever an appropriate opportunity presents itself.***

I strongly advocate that anyone who aspires to greatness in sales must truly commit to thoroughly mastering these skills. It's also imperative that you initially achieve a solid foundation of fundamental selling skills before you try to integrate some of the more advanced techniques into your repertoire. This is best accomplished by focusing on each individual chapter as a stand-alone training module. As in military basic training, a trainee must initially master individual skills such as marksmanship, combat tactics, physical fitness, etc., which collectively contribute to being a professional soldier.

You must also grasp how the individual elements of *The Sales Track* relate to the overall sales process. Each successive step builds on and validates the previous one, thereby collectively leading to the desired outcome.

The skills development exercises prescribed in this

workbook are an important part of you comprehending and internalizing these fundamentals. I urge you to make the effort to complete these exercises and periodically review and revise them as needed. Even for you seasoned, experienced sales reps, your sales instincts can dull over time and need to be rehoned. If you're willing to go to the gym to work out daily, why not also engage in some mental aerobics to rejuvenate your sales approach and overall presentation with some creative, new ideas?

As you read through the following chapters discussing *The Sales Track*, please recognize that the terms "prospect" and "customer" are used interchangeably. A prospect would typically be someone who you have not done business with before. A customer, on the other hand, would be an established account. However, as used herein, even an existing customer who you're trying to sell a new product to or expand their program would still be treated the same as a new prospect. The need to employ these effective selling techniques has the same significance to the outcome.

The "Sales Track" Concept

The remainder of this training manual will address all the steps of *The Sales Track* in the order they're shown. Bear in mind that the length of each step, its content, and sometimes even the order of each step can vary depending on the prospect and their particular circumstances. "Objections," for example, are free rovers and can occur anywhere in the sales presentation. The chapter on Objections in this workbook will arm you with techniques for effectively overcoming these.

There will frequently be some overlap in the sales steps and even some requirements to introduce items out of their normal sequence. This is pretty much dictated by your prospect's demeanor. Some prospects are very patient and considerate about allowing you to direct the flow of the presentation. Others want you to quickly get to the point. Obviously, it shouldn't come across as an interrogation session because that doesn't create a favorable selling atmosphere. Ideally, it should be perceived by the prospect as an exploratory discussion about their needs, concerns, problems, desires, preferences, etc.

Fundamentals of Selling

During the diagnosing phase, the prospect's answer to one of your questions may prompt you to then explain how a specific benefit relates to the need or concern just expressed. Even though you presented this benefit somewhat prematurely, it was appropriate to the logical flow of the presentation. Such instances become building blocks of the foundation you are laying for desire and conviction. The prospect's initial state of mind can also be a significant factor that will dictate how you should make your approach. A prospect can be any one of the following:

Sympathetic   Indifferent   *Hostile

*(*Not necessarily hostile at you personally, but rather at their particular circumstances.)*

The sympathetic buyer could be so as a result of responding to your company's advertising, or they might be a referral from a satisfied customer. The indifferent buyer, on

The "Sales Track" Concept

the other hand, is simply not sure at the onset if he should be receptive to your approach or not. The hostile prospect can be most challenging and demands careful diplomacy on your part.

The section on "disarming techniques" later in the workbook can be a big help in dealing with a hostile prospect. Each prospect or buyer is unique in how they must be sold. The old-fashioned canned sales pitch definitely won't work for the vast majority of today's consumers and businesses. Professional salespeople today have to be highly skilled in quickly assessing exactly how they need to sell a given prospect and adjusting their strategy accordingly.

As much as I've admired and benefitted from the books of renowned sales trainers myself, I've come to the conclusion that some of the old methods simply aren't as effective in today's information overload society. Today's consumer is very sophisticated and well informed. Instant access to virtually unlimited resources on the Internet has empowered and emboldened today's consumers. They're not as apt to be persuaded simply by a salesperson's assertiveness and persistence. They're also not as easily intimidated by the full-court press that used to be the mainstay of the strong-arm-style closers.

Today, believability must be the cornerstone for both the seller and the buyer. That's not to say that you don't have to contend with buyer reluctance. This is still selling, after all. However, the techniques presented in this manual will help you effectively deal with this. Just be sure that you temper your tactics with a commitment toward the credibility of your sales proposals. Frame your sales points in terms of how they serve the buyer's interests and not just yours. I'm reminded of the excellent advice given by Dr. Stephen Covey in his book, *The 7 Habits of Highly Effective People,* when he stated, "Seek first to understand, then to be understood."

If you have responsibility at your company for designing and administering a sales training program, then use *The Sales Track* as your framework. Personalize these steps to your particular product and selling environment. Engage your trainees as well as experienced reps in helping

The "Sales Track" Concept

devise effective sales tactics and strategies that they feel confident with in their sales realm. Then, constantly revisit these concepts to further refine and improve the effectiveness of your training program.

Training for any worthwhile endeavor is a never-ending process. Constantly strive to seek out new and creative ways to improve upon your skills. If you are a sales manager or sales trainer, I urge you to use *The Sales Track* as a blueprint for building an outstanding training program at your company. It can also increase your effectiveness when you make learning fun! The Sales Track board game that is available for download off our website with the purchase of this manual is a creative way to incorporate some of this fun into your training.

> **"Seek first to understand, then to be understood."**
>
> Dr. Stephen Covey,
> *The 7 Habits of Highly Effective People*

NOTES

SalesCadre.com

Chapter 3

The Approach
You Can't Sell 'Em if They
Won't Let You Tell 'Em!

An effective sales approach, simply put, must quickly create a favorable climate for the selling process to begin. Your opening statement (after introducing yourself) must be carefully conceived and designed to either ***spark interest*** or ***arouse curiosity*** and thereby ***render the prospect receptive to further sales dialogue***. Your skill in executing this will be the key to taking your prospect seamlessly from the "attention" phase into the "interest" phase (see the "Sales Track").

If you fail to successfully do this, the prospect can, and frequently will, quickly seize control and abruptly block your attempts to proceed further. This is where you typically hear the dreaded "I wouldn't be interested" response, and suddenly you're on the defensive instead of the offensive. Because of this built-in defense reaction that most people have to a sales approach, you must always be cognizant of this critical rule.

> **Always design your approach so that it does not easily lend itself to a response of "I wouldn't be interested."**

How do you go about doing this? For starters, operate from the perspective of how the prospect can benefit by granting you an audience and some of their valuable time. Let me give you some examples. Suppose you sell handheld wireless order entry devices. Your opening statement could be, "Mr. Smith, our compact wireless order entry device was designed with cost savings and ease of use in mind by simplifying order processing while increasing speed and accuracy. Is there any reason you wouldn't at least want to take a look at a system like

The Approach

that?" You should, of course, have a demo unit of your order entry device in your hand at this moment.

As you can see, such an opening does not *easily lend itself* to a response of "I wouldn't be interested." This particular example is actually based on a simple formula that can be used for almost all of your selling approaches. The formula is, "Mr. Prospect, our (Product or Service) was designed with (Benefit) in mind by (Performance Feature) while (Performance Feature)."

Even if your approach elicits an "I'm not interested" response, your next follow-up should be something like, "I can understand why you might feel that way, and perhaps this isn't for you. You know, Acme Labs, Criterion, and Atlas Chemical all initially felt the same way when I first approached them. But here's what they've found since switching to our device." This drop back maneuver allows you to regain the offensive and continue with your sales presentation. It also employs a tried-and-proven technique for handling objections known as the "Feel–Felt–Found" formula, which is discussed in greater detail in our "Objections Handling" chapter.

For added impact, you should also design a standard "Feature & Benefit" list as a visual piece to show the prospect at this moment to further reinforce your case.

Here's another example. A copier salesman hands the prospect two examples of letterhead done on linen finish bond paper and asks, "Can you tell which one of these was done by a commercial printer and which was done on a Focus Premier copier? If I could show you how you could produce quality copies like these for less than you're spending at a printer, is there any reason you wouldn't consider that?"

It's very important that you remember this rule regarding the sales approach: **Never get complacent about anticipating initial buyer resistance.** If you do, you risk wasting a viable prospect because you got caught with your guard down. I would compare it to a boxer going into the opening round with both fists down at his side. What do you think would probably happen? Always anticipate the possibility of buyer resistance and be prepared with well thought out and continuously refined comebacks. Please understand that I'm not advocating developing your verbal combative skills but rather grasping the importance of mental preparedness.

Pause for the Skills Development Exercise on the next page.

Skills Development Exercise

Design at least two approach statements involving your product or service that conform to the "Mr. Prospect, our (Product or Service) was designed with (Benefit) in mind by (Performance Feature) while (Performance Feature) formula."

The Approach

On some occasions, encountering initial resistance or rejection may simply be the result of bad timing on your part. The prospect may have a more pressing issue or crisis to deal with than your sales incursion. Consequently, you get the "I'm not interested," even though you opened with a well thought out interest creating remark. Sometimes a diplomatic retreat is the better part of valor. You can politely exit and regroup at some later date.

If, however, you sense that the prospect might maintain civility and perhaps even be conciliatory if you pressed a little further, you can try a low-key comeback like this. "Wow, that's got to be one of the quickest turndowns I've ever gotten. You must have some pretty strong reasons for not wanting to consider this now." Then just shut up and wait for the prospect's response. It will frequently reveal the underlying reason(s) for the prospect stonewalling your approach. When it does so, you then have an objection or concern that you can deal with.

If this isn't successful in gaining you an opening, then simply say, "I understand" and exit politely. Don't get defensive, indignant, or confrontational or you'll just contaminate the well. Thank them for their time and consideration and leave your business card. Some circumstances merit retreat and recontact at a more appropriate time.

> **When making your approach, always keep your guard up!**

As you'll see later in this chapter, your "arouse interest" opening remark(s) don't necessarily have to focus initially on your product or service. They can address a peripheral problem or concern that your product/service can resolve. An example of this type approach would be, "A recent *Wall Street Journal* survey[2] revealed that shipping errors and returns cost businesses on average two percent of their annual sales revenues. How have you been able to reconcile that within your operation?" Once again, I

---

[2] This fictitious survey is for illustrative purposes only and was not an actual survey conducted by the *Wall Street Journal*. Such trade publications articles are known as "validation" articles.

The Approach

emphasize the critical requirement that your approach should not easily lend itself to a response of "I wouldn't be interested."

I think it's also important that you clearly understand the prospect/buyer's perspective as you initiate your approach. I truly believe that most sales prospects really want to be considerate. Even those who reject your initial opening usually do so in an impersonal manner while trying not to seem hostile or wanting to hurt your feelings. They simply have this built-in defense to suddenly being thrust into a sales situation where they feel they're unprepared to make a prudent buying decision. We all do. Consequently, they'll throw out excuses (as opposed to objections) that are strictly intended to derail your sales approach.

Think about how you typically prefer to avoid salespeople when you're in an electronics store (e.g., Best Buy) and you just want to look and ponder the possibility of a major purchase without a salesperson engaging you in a sales situation. This is the essence of the "I'm just looking" defense to sales incursions. As a professional salesperson, you should anticipate this mindset and always be prepared for it. Learning to effectively deal with this commonly encountered sales hurdle must be a primary objective if you are to succeed on a high level in sales. Take care not to treat this challenge with contempt, but rather with an understanding of the underlying psychology.

As consumers, we all instinctively exhibit this trait. Pursue your sales efforts as Teddy Roosevelt might have: "Speak softly but carry a big stick." The stick would be your arsenal of selling skills, plus your extensive product knowledge. These in proper balance can lead a reluctant prospect into a mutually favorable selling situation.

Probably the most critical factor in how successful your routine approach will be is whether you yourself consider it believable. If it feels contrived or manipulative to you, then your lack of sincerity and genuineness will be evident to your prospect. Keep tweaking the wording of your approach until it feels right to you and you're confident

The Approach

using it. Recognize the fact that most prospective buyers feel they're entitled to exalted status in a selling situation. After all, you solicited them (in most cases) and not vice versa. It's your responsibility to sell the sale.

Pause for the Skills Development Exercise on the next page.

Skills Development Exercise

Design at least two approach statements (similar to the shipping errors and returns approach just mentioned) that focus on peripheral problems or concerns that your product/service resolves.

The Approach

How Creative Thinking Broke Down the Barrier

In 1981, I was director of marketing and training for an interconnect telephone company located in Tampa, Florida. We specialized in selling multi-line/multi-extension phone systems to small and medium sized businesses. This was shortly after the phone industry was forced to deregulate and as a provision of that had to divest themselves of renting and leasing telephones to businesses and consumers. Consequently, most businesses and consumers were suddenly forced to shop for their telephones. The major phone companies cleverly circumvented this change by establishing separate (unregulated) subsidiaries to sell, rent, or lease telephones. These new subsidiaries were intentionally given similar names to the phone company so as to give the public the impression that business remained as usual.

However, the fact of the matter was that businesses were put into the situation of having to make a buying decision regarding their phone systems even though many didn't fully grasp this. With our original approach strategy, we kept encountering businesses that had the misconception that they would be able to continue renting their phones through the "phone company." This led to a lot of "we're not interested," or "we're already set" responses that derailed our opening attempts to explain what deregulation truly meant for them.

After much contemplation, we came up with the following approach question. "Have you made a decision yet on who you'll be buying your phones from?" The beauty of this approach was that it instantly aroused curiosity if for no other reason than the prospect wanted to try to understand just what the heck we were talking about. This played right into our hands because the primary local newspaper, the *Tampa Tribune*, had recently published an article about deregulation with a headline that read something like "Deregulation Forces Businesses to Make Phone Buying Decision." The added impact and validation that this visual piece afforded us almost always worked to get us

The Approach

into our sales presentation with the prospect. Now we were in a position to explain what the prospect's options *really were* and how our company could meet their needs, usually with better equipment at a lower cost than they had been paying the phone company.

This example truly illustrates the essence of a well thought out approach strategy. We even added some additional visual impact by wearing buttons on our shirts that simply stated, "It's Coming! Are You Ready?" This visual teaser button further supported our efforts to get us into a sales dialogue with prospects. My point here is that you must be creative and innovative in devising your approach. This example certainly met the criteria that your approach must not easily lend itself to a response of, "I wouldn't be interested." Make yourself stand out from your competition—try something different, innovative, and creative. Think outside the box and have some fun doing so.

The Added Impact of a Visual Piece

Another effective deregulation approach strategy used by the alternative long-distance providers such as MCI and Sprint was to immediately hand the prospect examples of two mocked up phone bills. One looked like the incumbent phone company's bill listing all the long-distance calls and their respective costs and the total amounts for the month. The other showed a mocked up MCI (or Sprint) bill with the same long-distance calls and their lower prices. The salesperson's opening remark (after the introduction) was, "If I could make your long-distance phone bill look more like this instead of this, is there any reason you wouldn't at least want to consider that?"

This same visual piece price comparison concept is transferrable to numerous sales situations. An energy-reduction equipment salesperson shows an incumbent power company bill before their equipment's installation and after the installation highlighting the savings. Such engaging visual approaches can be extremely effective at

The Approach

gaining you an audience.

A person selling intangibles such as annuities could use the following approach. He shows the prospect a picture of a Starbucks grande latte and asks the following question: "If I could show you how to turn five of these a week into a monthly check like this for the rest of your life, is there any reason that wouldn't appeal to you?" Here again, the mocked up check easily created on a computer would have great visual and psychological impact in sparking interest. You could even add a little flair by actually writing the prospect's name into the "Payee" line on the check as you asked the question. This creative approach certainly has the power to create a favorable climate for the selling process to begin. See the footnote[3] below for an explanation of this logic if you're unfamiliar with annuities.

---

[3] This scenario assumes a weekly cost of five Starbucks grande lattes to be $20, or approximately $87 monthly. If this amount were invested in an annuity paying 6% interest compounded annually for 20 years, then the monthly payout starting at age 62 @ 6% return would provide a monthly check of approximately $275.

Another example of creative thinking occurred to me as a Yellow Pages sales rep in Tampa. When we received our account assignments for a given city, I would usually do a drive through over the weekend to scout out my new territory just to see what types of businesses I'd be calling on. One was a furniture store that had been in business over 30 years in the same location. They had just completed a major facelift of the front of their building. Since I routinely carried my camera with me on these scouting runs, I took some pictures of the attractive new storefront. I then designed a larger display ad for this customer than he was currently running and actually pasted it over his existing ad in my sales demo copy of the Tampa Yellow Pages directory. The new, larger ad prominently featured his new storefront in the center of the display ad.

When I arrived for my appointment to handle this account's advertising for the next year's phone book, the owner told me just to continue with what he had in the current directory. Upon hearing this, I opened my Tampa

The Approach

phone book and showed him the new ad I had created for him and said, "I think your attractive new storefront will drive a lot of new customers into your showroom."

He looked at me and asked, "How did you do that?"

With this "spark interest/arouse curiosity" maneuver, I instantly created a favorable setting to launch into my proposal about how this larger and more attractive ad could bring him new customers. He wound up approving the new larger display ad. Obviously this particular sales strategy is very unique to print advertising sales. My point, however, is you should devise creative ways to spark interest regardless of your product or service. I know it's an overused adage, but it's definitely applicable here. ***Think outside the box!***

Pause for the Skills Development Exercise on the next page.

Skills Development Exercise

Design at least two approaches that incorporate the use of a visual piece (relative to your product or service) to engage your prospect in dialogue similar to the MCI phone bill or copier linen bond comparison examples.

Develop two ideas for "spark interest/arouse curiosity" buttons that are relevant to your specific selling situation.

SalesCadre.com

The Approach

The Best Sales Comeback Ever— The *"Stun Statement"*

Early in my sales career, I was fortunate enough to encounter a sales manager who gave me probably the most effective sales comeback I've ever used. He described it as a "Stun Statement," and it can be used to counter quite a few different sales approach rejections. Here's an example.

"Mr. Prospect, our new web-based inventory management system can virtually eliminate the hassles typically associated with this function while reducing costs. Is there any reason you wouldn't at least want to take a look at something like that?"

Prospect: "We just bought a new computer system which handles our inventory management, so I wouldn't be interested."

Your Stun Statement response: **"That's exactly why I'm here."** The beauty of this response is that it momentarily stuns the prospect and puts him or her into a state of at least curiosity, if not interest. It doesn't challenge or take issue with their position. Their built-in defense mechanism is temporarily disabled, thereby giving you an opening. Then you simply explain how your product/service *complements* their new computer system, rather than trying to replace or compete with it. It's important that your stun statement be delivered not in a challenging tone, but rather in a pleasant, confident manner that conveys a genuine focus on supporting their needs. This response can thereby lend itself to a variety of prospect comebacks to your approach.

For example:

- We've already finalized our advertising campaign for the year. Your response: **"That's exactly why I'm here."**
- We've never relied on outside contractors to support our service department. **"That's exactly why I'm here."**
- We did business with your company a few years

ago and the results were terrible. **"That's exactly why I'm here."**

- We've never found a vendor that could integrate successfully with our system. **"That's exactly why I'm here."**

- We're happy with our current supplier. **"That's exactly why I'm here."**

Because this last example is so common to a variety of sales situations, let me offer some examples of how to follow up after deploying your stun statement.

(1) "Just as a routine health exam is a good idea from time to time, it's also good to periodically revalidate crucial business decisions. Although I certainly wouldn't expect to displace your current supplier on the spot, there may come a time when you need to consider a replacement supplier or at least a supplemental one. Unexpected events can disrupt or alter a smooth-running relationship and jeopardize your service capabilities. Let me just share with you a checklist of capabilities that top-notch

suppliers are offering these days." (You should have this visual piece already prepared and readily at hand.) NOW, this should gain you an audience, so go sell 'em!

(2) Here's a variation on the above: "I'm sure I'm not the first salesperson who's come in here promising to save you money or drastically improve your operation, but just consider this. At one time, even your best supplier was an untried vendor to you that showed up making similar claims, right?"

(3) An adjunct to the above maneuver is to pursue the "backup supplier" strategy. It goes something like this: "Mr. Prospect, even the best suppliers occasionally fumble the ball, oftentimes through no fault of their own. A great way to minimize such disruptions to your service is to develop some backup supplier relationships. It's really a no-lose proposition since the backup candidate will be anxious to prove their worth to you. Give them your hard-to-resolve cases like temporary stock-outs or non-standard items and test drive their performance. Then, if they fail to deliver or perform poorly, they realize that

The Approach

their chances of ever becoming your primary supplier are pretty much trashed."

This strategy then sets the stage for you to move into the "diagnosing" phase of your presentation. You could ask such questions as, "Are you currently experiencing any stock-outs or unavailability of certain items you routinely get requests for?" "What are some of the most important capabilities you look for when evaluating prospective suppliers?" "A well thought out contingency plan sure beats recurring crisis management, wouldn't you agree?" The possibilities with this are virtually endless. You simply need to be well prepared with your supporting arguments once this stunner gains you your opening.

The power of the Stun Statement.
"That's Exactly Why I'm Here!"

Although I realize that these examples may not precisely fit every reader's situation, my point is to be creative in formulating your approach. The recurring theme is that the approach must be designed in such a way as to not easily elicit a response of "I wouldn't be interested." If you find that you're experiencing a high percentage of "I wouldn't be interested" responses to your approach, then it's obviously not working for you. It needs to be revised and tweaked until you routinely succeed in sparking interest or arousing curiosity and thus create a favorable situation to initiate your sales dialogue.

Also, recognize as in the previous examples that your approach should be one of calm, confident, and thought-provoking dialogue, rather than challenging, confrontational, or overbearing in demeanor. I strongly urge you to complete the "Skills Development Exercise" following this chapter to personalize several approach ideas for your particular selling circumstances. Remember that the returns you can expect from this training manual will be directly proportionate to the effort you put into it.

Pause for the Skills Development Exercise on the next page.

Skills Development Exercise

Develop a "Backup Supplier" strategy approach suitable for your particular product or service.

The Telephone Approach

Prospecting by phone or trying to set appointments over the phone is still an integral part of most outside sales jobs. It just comes with the territory. Security concerns today, however, have made this task extremely challenging. Voice mail has become a virtual firewall to filter the deluge of solicitations that businesses receive daily. It's even difficult to just drop by a place of business anymore and gain access to their lobby without a preset appointment. You definitely face a tough predicament because in order to set an appointment, you need to know the name of the individual with whom you wish to meet.

Because telephone prospecting really doesn't constitute a step in *The Sales Track* as presented herein, I'm merely going to relate how professional selling skills must be employed in this type of approach. There are numerous articles on telephone prospecting available that address this topic more in-depth than I do here. An excellent website for this is www.SellingPower.com.

The Approach

Obviously, the first thing you have to do is uncover the name of the primary individual you need to target. As mentioned above, today's security-conscious society makes this very challenging. Many company websites will list some of their corporate executives. Start with these names and try to drill down to the individual you're seeking. You can also research companies on Hoovers.com. By calling the company's main switchboard number, you can ask for one of these executives by name and then possibly be offered the opportunity to dial another extension for their assistant. By using a cordial and humble approach of "I was hoping you might be able to help me out," I've frequently extracted the name and direct phone number of the person I really need to target from their assistant.

If you wind up in voice mail, however, you must leave a brief but compelling message that invites a response. For example, I might employ this type of voice mail message to try to elicit a callback. "A recent change in FTC rules has significantly impacted virtually everyone in your industry. You may not be fully informed on how this could potentially disrupt your operations. If you'd like to receive a recent trade magazine article about this issue, please call me at _____ or e-mail me at _____. This is Jim Norred with Dynamics Systems."

As you can see, my message was carefully designed to spark interest or arouse enough curiosity to result in a callback or e-mail. In fact, the product or service was not even mentioned nor does it necessarily need to be in a voice mail message. Remember, your mission is to secure an appointment, not to make a sale at this juncture.

In formulating your approach message, make it as concise as possible while also being compelling and engaging. This is true whether you get a live prospect on the phone or wind up in their voice mail. You only have about 20 seconds to arouse interest or spark enough curiosity to gain you an appointment or callback. The same rule applies here as in your face-to-face sales approach. Design your approach in such a way that it does not easily lend

The Approach

itself to a response of "I wouldn't be interested."

Pause for the Skills Development Exercise on the next page.

Skills Development Exercise

Design at least two telephone approaches that focus on peripheral problems or concerns that your product/service addresses (similar to the Dynamics Systems approach).

SalesCadre.com

The Approach

The "Gatekeeper"

The old "secretarial barrier" or gatekeeper, as they were often called, has also been rendered virtually irrelevant by today's security measures. You're pretty unlikely to encounter a protective secretary if you don't already have a prearranged appointment. This may occur today, however, if you make cold calls on small businesses that only have a few employees. In such instances, the old techniques are still applicable. Your objective is to courteously obtain information about the business and determine with whom you need to meet.

As in the past, this frequently elicits a response from the secretary of "May I ask what this is regarding?" The recommended strategy for dealing with this is to respond with a question that the secretary would be reluctant to answer because they aren't knowledgeable enough about the issue. For example, you respond to "May I ask what this is regarding?" with "Yes, can you tell me how much maintenance downtime you're currently experiencing on your primary servers?" Your question should, of course, have direct relevance to the merits of your particular product or service. The key to such a response's effectiveness is that it will generally get you referred to the primary decision maker because the secretary doesn't feel qualified to answer that particular question. As I've stressed so often in this manual, you must continually tweak these types of approaches until you find the one that routinely works for you.

In all cases involving the secretary or receptionist, treat them with the respect their position demands. They can't say yes, but they can deny you access if your approach isn't professional and considerate.

Pause for the Skills Development Exercise
on the next page

Skills Development Exercise

Design at least two "secretarial barrier" questions (relative to your particular product or service) that would result in you successfully extracting the name of the appropriate decision maker for you to target.

SalesCadre.com

NOTES

SalesCadre.com

Chapter 4

Effective Diagnosing

As *The Sales Track* graphic indicates, "diagnosing" is the next logical step after you have successfully established a favorable situation for the selling process to begin. This means that you have either sparked interest or aroused curiosity on the part of the prospect.

Note also in *The Sales Track* graphic that the prospect's state of mind should now be receptive for you to begin building their desire. This is predicated on you accurately identifying what motive(s) would most likely influence your prospect to act favorably on your recommendations. This is a critical step requiring that you employ keen analytical skills without appearing like you're conducting an interrogation session.

Obviously, some preliminary deliberation should go into accurately identifying your target prospect's profile. As the old saying goes, it's ridiculous to try to sell air conditioners to Eskimos, regardless of how great the product is. That being said, the diagnosing techniques presented herein presuppose that you are pursuing viable prospects for your particular product or service. Some products and services, such as copiers, have very broad appeal. Others, e.g. medical instruments, are much narrower in their market focus. Your diagnosing skills are best directed at prospects that typically have the need, desire, means, and reason to buy your product or service.

The art of inquiry is the cornerstone of an effective sales presentation. This is accomplished through the use of some tried-and-proven questions designed specifically to identify needs, desires, problems, etc., that can be plausibly related to your product or service's benefits. As you do this, however, it's important to remember that what *you* feel are the most compelling reasons for someone to buy your product may not necessarily be the same for the

Effective Diagnosing

prospect. Your diagnosing must uncover the prospect's predominant buying motive(s) and do so in a reasonable period of time. Their interest level will quickly wane in the absence of relevant and engaging questions.

Because buying is typically emotionally driven, your presentation must appeal to what sparks *their* interest. It's a fact that people are much more likely to buy something they *want* than something they *need*. Prospects don't just buy your product or service; they buy what your product or service will do for them.

Buying motives generally fall under one of the following three influences: PRIDE – PROFIT – PROTECTION. These motives don't necessarily have to be rational. For example, a person doesn't pay $20,000 for a Audemars Piguet™ or Breitling™ wristwatch because they want to be sure their timepiece is extremely accurate. They do it because of the prestige (or pride) the brand affords them. Similarly, people don't buy a liability insurance policy primarily because of their concern over people getting hurt on their property, but rather, to protect their personal assets in the event that someone does.

As mentioned earlier, an important element of effective diagnosing techniques is to show genuine interest in what's important to the prospect. This is because many prospects are reluctant to be forthcoming in providing information. This goes back to their built-in resistance to being sold something. You can counter this resistance by asking the right questions and listening intently to the responses.

It's not that different from the methods used by a physician. Without a thorough and accurate diagnosis, you can't adequately prescribe an effective remedy. You'll be surprised at how open prospects will be when you show that you clearly want to understand their perspective. If you sell to businesses as opposed to consumers, you'll also find that prospects are impressed when you demonstrate that you've taken the time to research their company, product, industry, and history.

Consequently, the opening questions you ask can really

Effective Diagnosing

set the tone for productive conversation. As an example, a universal diagnosing opening might be, "What's the secret to succeeding in your type of business?" This engaging question invites dialogue that most prospects feel flattered to respond to, rather than feeling they're just feeding you information to serve your sales efforts. Here are some other effective diagnosing questions and openings:

- What are some of the biggest challenges you face in your job?
- What considerations are most important to you when evaluating a potential new supplier or product line?
- What are some of the critical issues your company faces today?
- What do you feel needs to happen to get you where you want to be?
- What would you like to improve about the way you currently handle your _____?

- How has your company tried to cope with recurring technical obsolescence of your _____ equipment?

- How have you been able to reconcile escalating costs without raising prices to your customers?

- To what would you attribute your company's steady growth?

- Since I don't want to profess to be an expert about your business and its unique needs, why don't you tell me what's important to you?

As you develop your diagnosing skills, it's important to clearly understand just how critical the wording of a probing question is to the results it's likely to produce. A poorly worded question can lead to a dead end, whereas a skillfully devised question can be an opportunity on-ramp.

The examples given in the previous paragraph were all opportunity on-ramp type questions because they were designed to elicit information critical to making the sale. To cite an example for comparison, a dead end question

Effective Diagnosing

would be, "Do you project any major equipment purchases in the next 12 – 18 months?" An opportunity on-ramp question, on the other hand, would be, "What profit improvement or cost reduction areas will your company be focusing on in the next 12 – 18 months?" Effective diagnosing is not simply a matter of random interrogation. It's skillfully formulating astute follow up questions based on relevant information that you've extracted from the prospect. I urge you to complete the skills development exercises in this chapter to help you refine your diagnosing techniques with respect to question structure.

When I sold Yellow Pages advertising, one of my favorite diagnosing openers was, "How do you go about trying to attract new customers?" The variety of responses I received almost invariably provided me with clues to how I should formulate my sales strategy. This type of question is the essence of effective diagnosing.

All of the above dialogue starters are designed to draw the prospects out and invite them to reveal what would motivate them to buy. At this stage of the selling process, you're still formulating your recommendations based on the feedback you elicit from the prospect. This process is ANALYZE—then STRATEGIZE (your desire and conviction-building responses)—then CRYSTALLIZE the concept, first in your mind, and then in the prospect's mind. The concept as used here is how you ultimately determine you can meet the prospects' needs, solve their problems, or fulfill their desires.

In order to excel at this phase, you must also master the art of correctly using and integrating the right mix of "open-ended" questions with "closed-ended" questions. Here are examples of both types:

OPEN-ENDED: "What do you feel are the biggest obstacles to upgrading your distribution center this year?" Open-ended questions are intended to be more thought provoking and, thus allow more leeway for the prospect to respond. Consequently, you have less control in directing the course of where their response might lead.

CLOSED-ENDED: "How many copies do you generally

Effective Diagnosing

run a day?" Closed-ended questions call for shorter, more precise answers and can even be simple yes or no questions. They afford you greater control in directing the course of the interview.

Another technique you can use to draw prospects into revealing clues to their buying motives is to use the bracketing method of questioning. An example would be, "Bill, most of the companies we talk to about our innovative new __(Product or Service)__ are primarily concerned with three main areas: price, serviceability, and ease of use. How does that equate with your situation?"

The criterion for effective diagnosing questions is that they must elicit the true reasons why a prospect might favorably consider your recommendation(s). Properly designing your questions will produce these results. They may also uncover buyer concerns or objections which need to be effectively dealt with as they arise. Armed with this information, you can begin to facilitate a buying decision based on motives the prospect has revealed to you.

Permit me to reiterate again that effective diagnosing should be less like an interrogation and more like a discussion about the prospects' needs, concerns, desires, problems, preferences, etc. You can then help them discover and ultimately agree upon a solution that they feel good about. I repeat again the sound advice given by Dr. Stephen Covey in his book, *The 7 Habits of Highly Effective People*, where he stated, "Seek first to understand, then to be understood."

Pause for the Skills Development Exercise on the next page.

Effective Diagnosing

Skills Development Exercise

Design some "opportunity on-ramp" questions that can be your default diagnosing dialogue starters.

Design a "bracketing" diagnosing question that is suitable to your particular product or service.

People don't buy your product or service; they buy what your product or service will do for them!

NOTES

Chapter 5

Presenting with Benefits Builds Desire & Creates Conviction

The opening page of this book showcases a statement in bold print that reads, "Selling is knowing what to say, how to say it, and when to say it." A bit oversimplified perhaps, but that really is the essence of selling. This chapter on Presenting with Benefits requires that we very closely examine the salesperson's actions with the corresponding prospect's state of mind. In this phase, you must build desire and ultimately create conviction in the mind of the prospect. Accomplishing this is dependent upon how effectively you relate your sales presentation to the buying motives uncovered in the previous diagnosing phase.

I'm reminded of a slight variation on a quote made

famous by an eighteenth-century British politician and poet.[4] The variation is, "The object of oratory is not to educate, but to persuade." This certainly has relevance to selling in the sense that a well-informed prospect that elects not to buy generally was not adequately *persuaded* by your presentation. This is why providing product knowledge without employing effective selling skills is pure recital that produces no results beyond educating. Therefore, let's consider some important pointers.

- Know your product thoroughly, but remember that if people only bought based on product performance specifications and features, then a well designed brochure could replace most salespeople. You must also exhibit enthusiasm during your presentation. You can't really expect to ignite enthusiasm in your prospect if it's barely flickering in you.

- Don't stress too much over memorizing a sales

---

[4] Thomas Babington Macaulay was a British politician, historian, and poet. His exact quote was, "The object of oratory alone is not truth, but persuasion."

script because it tends to produce more anxiety than results. It's better to create an outline of your sales presentation that you can use as a guide. A well designed sales visual can then serve to highlight the key points of your presentation. Review it with the prospect in a natural, unscripted manner. Remember, while you're covering these key sales points with the prospect, you must also be actively listening to his or her comments. They can provide you with the clues to creating desire, conviction, and ultimately, how to successfully close the sale.

- Although I don't advocate memorizing a sales script, there should be a core sales presentation that is essentially a brief overview of how and why your product or service satisfies a need. Keep in mind, of course, that this must be a *perceived need* from the *prospect's perspective*. In order to effectively create desire, you must ensure that you succeed in getting the prospects to acknowledge that they have a need, problem, or desire that your product/service can satisfy.

The prospects' perception of need is paramount here, not just yours. Do they clearly recognize that your proposal provides a solution, enhances their profit, prestige, efficiency, or security level? You should also avoid deluging your prospect with product specs and performance data unless they specifically relate to needs you've identified via your diagnosing. Think about the last time a car salesperson talked incessantly about a particular car's features without first determining what was important to you. I suspect that your interest subsided quickly.

As mentioned earlier, a well designed sales visual outlining key points is an effective way to ensure you cover critical sales points with a prospect. This is much preferred to the old "shoot from the hip" approach where you wing it on every call. Just remember that a sales visual is only intended to reinforce your presentation, not replace it.

I suggest that you write out your basic default presentation and then record it (as an MP3) so you can listen to it as you drive. You should revise and tweak it periodically

Presenting with Benefits Builds Desire & Creates Conviction

and try to get the fundamental idea ingrained into your memory. It's not necessary or even recommended that you memorize it verbatim. Use the "Sales Call Evaluation" form in the back of this workbook to provide you with input and ideas to improve this core presentation. It's from within this presentation that you will be introducing the prospect-specific feature/benefit statements that gradually build conviction.

- Be careful that your sales presentation doesn't contain too much flash and not enough substance. An example of this might be a cell phone salesperson demonstrating how the camera function of the phone can actually allow onscreen editing of a photo. However, the sales rep failed to uncover that the prospect's primary interest was in the calling and e-mail capabilities of the phone. Just because you're intrigued with a cell phone that can remotely lower a home heating system's thermostat doesn't necessarily mean a prospect will be. This simply reemphasizes the point that effectively diagnosing is an indispensable prerequisite to this stage of the Sales Track.

- Be sure that you clearly understand the difference between a feature and a benefit. A feature is a design or performance specification of your product or service. A benefit is the value delivered by that feature as perceived by its recipient. For example, a feature of a particular make and model automobile could be ABS brakes. The benefit of that feature to the vehicle's owner is increased safety. One of the best examples I ever heard a sales trainer give when explaining the difference between a feature and its corresponding benefit was dental braces. A person doesn't spend thousands of dollars with an orthodontist because they want the new almost invisible braces. They do so because they want beautiful-looking teeth.

Here's an effective formula for translating features into benefits that should become instinctive to you. The formula is **Because of** _____, **you can**

Presenting with Benefits Builds Desire & Creates Conviction

_____, **which means** _____.

Using this formula for our ABS brakes, the wording would be something like, "Because of the standard ABS brakes, you can stop quickly and confidently in all weather conditions, which means added safety for you and your family." Here's another automobile-related feature/benefit example. "Because of the 7-way adjustable driver's seat, it can be adjusted to any driver's exact comfort setting and stored in memory, which means no driver fatigue at the end of a long business trip."

The chapter on Diagnosing presented the ANALYZE—STRATEGIZE—CRYSTALLIZE formula that leads you into the presenting with benefits phase. The above examples would have been based upon information you obtained during your diagnosing. The clues you uncovered led you to strategize that a major concern of your prospect was (1) safety of the vehicle because of his two young children, and (2) that he also drives the vehicle on many long-distance business trips. Therefore, you crystallized these conclusions into the "because of, you can, which means" formula. This tactic is intended to build conviction in the prospect and thereby set the stage for the closing phase.

Pause for the Skills Development Exercise on the next page.

Presenting with Benefits Builds Desire & Creates Conviction

Skills Development Exercise

Using the formula "Because of _____, you can _____, which means _____," develop four feature/benefit translation statements relative to your product or service.

SalesCadre.com

Another sales trainer I had the pleasure of working with gave me a great idea for remembering to properly translate features into benefits for the prospect. He suggested that you envision a neon sign on the prospect's forehead that reads, "SO WHAT?" each time you mentioned a feature. That visualization proved to be very effective for me in my sales career. This can also be relevant to the prospect that has "no perceived need" and it's up to you to enlighten them. These are like those people who physically feel great but have an underlying medical problem that exhibits no evident symptoms.

Take, for example, long-term care insurance. Some people have the attitude that if their health ever deteriorated to the point where they needed to be put in a nursing home that they would refuse such treatment or just run away and disappear. Consequently, they deduce that long-term care insurance is an unnecessary expense for them. What they fail to recognize, however, is that their spouse, children, or siblings frequently wind up shouldering the burden of their decision and the corresponding

Presenting with Benefits Builds Desire & Creates Conviction

financial impact due to the onset of Alzheimer's or dementia. Once people grasp this potential repercussion to their family, they will generally perceive this need in a different light and, thus, be more receptive to long-term care insurance.

Although this argument is certainly rational, it can and must be portrayed as emotional as well. Very few people would want to inflict this kind of financial burden on their family if they had the means to prevent it. If you occasionally encounter this "no perceived need" obstacle to your sales efforts, then analyze, strategize, and crystallize a plan to overcome it.

Pause for the Skills Development Exercise on the next page.

Skills Development Exercise

Devise a strategy for dealing with those prospects you encounter that have no perceived need of your product or service. Write out the exact wording you would use to preempt this up front and overcome it with your prospect.

Presenting with Benefits Builds Desire & Creates Conviction

A concern I'd like to address before proceeding further is the notion some sales aspirants may have that professional selling is manipulative in nature. Although there are, regrettably, those salespeople who employ manipulative tactics to achieve results, it certainly isn't required or desired.

I recall working with some hotshot sales reps in my Yellow Pages days that would describe a just completed sale as, "Man, I really slammed that dude!" Such an arrogant, selfish attitude toward the prospect, in my opinion, is indicative of a salesperson who just doesn't get it. We referred to them as "schlock"[5] artists because their big, impressive sales usually unraveled at the first opportunity.

Verbally pummeling a prospect into submission is not professional selling, it's intimidation. Most of the time, when people cave in to high pressure sales tactics, they do so just so they can end the onslaught. Afterward,

---

[5] According to Wikipedia, "schlock" is an English word of Yiddish origin meaning something cheap, shoddy, or inferior. In the field of science (again, according to Wikipedia), schlock refers to shoddy or unreliable results.

they're resentful that they were strong armed into making a decision that they had not fully reconciled in their mind as being the right thing to do. Consequently, this resentment quickly turns into buyer's remorse, and the big sale gets cancelled.

I view a professional salesperson as a facilitator, not a manipulator. *Funk & Wagnall's Dictionary* defines facilitate as, "to make easier or more convenient." It defines manipulate as, "to manage shrewdly and deviously for one's own profit." I truly believe that professional salespeople help prospects/customers make decisions that they conclude will benefit them. It's not something that is contrived or coerced. Done properly and professionally, both parties feel good about the decision.

Many of the sales books I've read do not include "conviction" in their version of a logical sale's progression. Although the actual act of taking a prospect from desire to conviction is virtually seamless, I do feel it's an important and necessary evolution that must take place in the prospect's mind. The conviction step solidifies the

Presenting with Benefits Builds Desire & Creates Conviction

prospect's commitment to taking favorable action on your proposal.

Let me give you an example that illustrates my point. Over the years, I have developed a moderate hearing loss that affects my ability to clearly comprehend some conversations. Being in sales, this certainly became a growing concern on my part. After resisting looking into hearing aids for a long time, I finally decided to see a hearing specialist. This specialist confirmed that I had a moderate hearing loss and offered to let me wear a new, discreet, digital technology in-ear device for a week with no obligation to buy.

Although I experienced some noticeable improvement in my hearing (which I greatly desired), my hang-up over the stigma of wearing a hearing aid prevented me from buying one (thus, no conviction). What could have overcome this?

Probably for me, the device would have had to been virtually unnoticeable and unobtrusive, which it wasn't.

When it comes to conviction, just remember that there's a big difference between "gotta have" and "wanna have," or even possibly, "like to have." Insulin to a diabetic is not a discretionary purchase, whereas a larger, newer model of a wide-screen high-definition TV is.

As stated earlier, transitioning a prospect from desire into conviction is pretty much a seamless process. This is where you resolve any lingering reluctance the prospect may still have and commence to seal the deal in the prospect's mind.

How do you determine when to begin this transition? I believe that it's an instinct that you develop and improve upon with experience. Certainly the prospect's body language and demeanor should provide clues to you. Also, feedback that you've elicited from the prospect will tell you when it's time to solidify conviction and be alert to closing opportunities.

The proper use of "tie downs" will validate the prospect's conviction to both himself as well as to you. Tie downs

Presenting with Benefits Builds Desire & Creates Conviction

are short, simple questions you use immediately after presenting a benefit that confirms the prospect's acknowledgement of the value of that benefit. An example of a tie down would be, "Can you see how that would work well with your operation?"

Pause for the Skills Development Exercise
on the next page.

Skills Development Exercise

Design four default "tie downs" to routinely use when presenting benefit statements to your prospect.

Presenting with Benefits Builds Desire & Creates Conviction

Helping the prospect to visualize already owning and enjoying the benefits of your product/service is one of the best ways to build conviction. Let me give you an example. I've been car crazy ever since I was a kid. When I once went to look at a new Datsun (now known as Nissan) 300ZX sports car, it was fairly easy for the sales rep to ascertain that my interests were in racy-looking sports cars and not vans or 4-door sedans. However, I had fairly strong preconceived notions of what I did and didn't want in vehicle options and accessories.

Because I'm from the old school of automotive technology, I discounted the new high-tech digital dashes as being too flashy and not really the traditional analog gauges I preferred. The sales rep didn't have the exact color and transmission combination I wanted right then, so he promised to do a search and get back to me the next day. He located a gold 5-speed with T-tops; however, it came with the digital dash package.

Here's how he successfully sold me on it. He called mid-afternoon and asked if I could come by and check out the digital dash model he had brought over to his lot. Albeit reluctantly, I agreed to come by that evening around six thirty as he suggested. When we embarked on my test drive just as nightfall set in, that beautiful digital dash and stereo combination lit up in all its radiant beauty, and it just blew me away. He used the descriptive term "awesome" that was frequently cited by Datsun in their 300ZX magazine ads and TV commercials. He laid it on thicker by saying things like, "Just imagine what the ladies are going to think about this little beauty." Well, I was hooked and my transition from desire to conviction was seamlessly accomplished via this emotional and sensory visualization.

Folks, if that's not facilitating a purchase, I don't know what is. I left there in my new dream machine feeling great about my decision and how this salesman helped me to make it.

Recall the last time you made a discretionary purchase of something you didn't necessarily need, but definitely wanted. Take your first wide-screen high-definition LCD

Presenting with Benefits Builds Desire & Creates Conviction

or plasma TV, for example. You probably, like me, had been scoping them out for a while and resisting the salesperson's attempts to draw you into a sales situation. You know, you throw out the old "I'm just looking" defense. However, they probably employed a low-key approach tactic along the lines of, "We're offering free delivery and hookup on all 42 inch and larger models this week." This no-pressure enticement set the stage for further sales dialogue, although you still maintained your hesitancy to make the purchase right then.

As the sales rep skillfully executed her diagnosing and presenting with benefits, your desire level gradually grew. When she determined that one of your biggest interests was watching NFL football and she demonstrated a game on a particular model with excellent performance specs for sports broadcasts, you were blown away. She probably said something like, "Can you imagine what your buddies are going to say when they come over on Super Bowl Sunday and eyeball this bad boy?" Just remember that emotion usually trumps reason when it comes to overcoming buyer reluctance in this type scenario. Emotion is telegraphed not just by what the salesperson says, but also how she says it.

This well executed transition from building desire into conviction simply enabled you to make that buying decision without reservation. Another example would be when a realtor having determined that the prospect desired a swimming pool says something like this, "You could really have some great pool parties in this setting, right?" This strategy also relies on the infectiousness of the sales rep's enthusiasm and the transference of his excitement to you. The rep's carefully conceived, well-timed remarks help you feel good about making the purchase now.

Although these examples involve selling to consumers, the underlying psychology would be the same when selling to businesses. Business owners as well as their buyers need to feel confident that they are making the best decision overall. Your presentation must persuade them that you offer the best solution to their problem(s), enhancement

Presenting with Benefits Builds Desire & Creates Conviction

to their operation, security for their fears, profit improvement, prestige among their peers, competitive edge, etc. It's up to you to facilitate this happening. It hinges upon a well conceived sales strategy.

As you move into this phase, you must also be cognizant of the fact that objections most often surface during this stage. Anticipate frequently encountered objections and handle them in a cool, confident manner. Remember that at this point, objections simply signal that the prospect is seeking more reassurance that they're making the right decision. Now you should be well positioned to start attempting to close the sale.

Pause for the Skills Development Exercise on the next page.

Skills Development Exercise

Research and compile a list of web-based support resources that you can (potentially) incorporate into your sales presentation where appropriate. These can be YouTube videos, blog sites, hotlinks to relevant trade magazine articles, etc.

Chapter 6

Objections:

Obstacles or Opportunities?

As a sales professional, it's important to recognize and anticipate that you will probably encounter some level of resistance on practically every sales call you make. Such resistance from prospects may be legitimate concerns, or they may just be excuses or smoke screens. Overcoming prospect doubt and reluctance is a normal part of your sales job. It comes with the territory.

You may also recall from the chapter on The Sales Track that objections are free rovers. Even though they're depicted on *The Sales Track* graphic as falling between "Presenting with Benefits" and "Closing," they can occur anywhere in the sales process. Objections can potentially be the first response you hear from a prospect, so you must anticipate this possibility and be prepared to deal with it effectively.

Novice salespeople generally cringe when they encounter objections, whereas skilled professionals welcome them. They view them as signals along the sales track to keep themselves posted on the prospect's understanding of the recommendations, their inclinations, or reservations, and their overall attitude toward the proposal. Becoming adept at handling prospect objections is critical to your success in sales. Failing to master this skill will result in chronic frustration and numerous lost sales that could have otherwise been successfully concluded.

As with other aspects of the sales process, I feel it's important to understand the underlying psychology of objections from the prospect's perspective. Most people upon finding themselves in a sales situation where they sense they're being led toward making a decision they *may not* feel ready to make will activate their built-in defense. It doesn't necessarily mean that they don't want to

Objections: Obstacles or Opportunities?

buy. It simply means that they need to feel confident that this is the right decision for them and not just the salesperson. They may also feel a bit intimated by the salesperson's presentation skills and somewhat anxious about the salesperson's ability to counter any objections they may raise. This is why a calm, reassuring demeanor on the part of the salesperson helps to lower this innate buyer resistance.

Accept the fact that objections are usually a normal part of the buying process. They indicate that the prospect is actually considering your proposal and is simply seeking further clarification or reassurance. It should not be viewed as a contest of wills where verbally pummeling the prospect into submission is acceptable.

The downside of a combative response (among other things) is that it usually elevates the prospect's resistance level. Even if you succeed in securing an order under high-pressure duress, it generally produces buyer's remorse shortly after you've exited with your signed order. Keep in mind that most sales contracts are subject to Federal Trade

Commission law that grants a 72-hour window during which a sale can be cancelled by the consumer without penalty. Just remember the old adage that *a sale loosely woven will quickly unravel at the first opportunity.*

The following formula for effectively handling objections is a tried-and-proven method that's been taught by virtually all of the great sales trainers. Let me preface this by saying that you should welcome all objections with a calm and confident composure. Even under provocation, it is important that you not lose your cool and, thus, control of the interview. If you allow your emotional reaction to rejection short circuit your selling skills, you're in for a lot of frustration. Maintaining a pleasant and calm demeanor will frequently influence the prospect to be more considerate and receptive. Here's a great rule to always remember:

> **If you lose your Cool, you no longer Rule!**

Upon hearing "I wouldn't be interested," if you respond with something like, "Why? You got a thing against salespeople?" you relinquish your control of the interview. The prospect can now feel justified in rejecting your efforts to proceed further, and in most cases, they probably will. In effect, you would have just poisoned the pond for any future attempts to reopen a dialogue with this prospect. I frequently repeated the above slogan to myself before making a difficult call involving an irate customer. The "disarming" techniques discussed later in this chapter are definitely an effective countermeasure in such instances.

Overcoming Stalls & Objections

Definition of an "objection": "Reluctance or concern on the part of a prospect/customer regarding some element of your proposal." A "stall," on the other hand, is "an excuse for not wanting to deal with your sales attempt or proposal at the moment."

Example of an objection: "We've never contracted out any of our service work before."

Example of a stall: "I couldn't possibly consider such a proposal until after our budget is finalized."

Step # 1 – Listen carefully. Hear the prospect out!

Here it is *extremely* important to resist the urge to anticipate the objection and respond before the prospect has fully explained his objection. First of all, it's just common courtesy. Second, it shows genuine interest on your part and ensures that you get a clear understanding of the objection. The counterproductive habit of assuming you know the objection before the prospect has fully expressed it only serves to further raise the prospect's resistance level. This is because he sees that you're focused more on your rebuttal than his concern(s). I remind you again of Dr. Stephen Covey's advice, "Seek first to understand, then to be understood."

Step # 2 – Soften resistance.

This is where you inject the "Feel–Felt–Found" formula that I initially mentioned in the chapter on The Approach. What this allows you to do is exhibit empathy for the prospect. It actually lowers the prospect's resistance by acknowledging that he certainly has a right to feel the way he does. This technique, often referred to as "bridging," has the effect of softening the lead-in to your answer and making it less abrupt. It also affords you some time to carefully formulate your response so that it addresses the objection precisely.

Example: Prospect: "We never contract out any of our service work."

Your response: "I can certainly appreciate why you might **feel** that way. In fact, some of my best customers initially **felt** that same way too. However, what they **found** was … (state benefits)."

Step # 3 – Paraphrase, then convert the objection into

a question.

What you're trying to do in this step is to convert an objection that may seem argumentative into a question that invites an answer. Continuing with the above example: "If I understand you correctly, Bill, you have some doubts that contract service can meet the high standards your company prides itself on while making financial sense as well. Is that reasonably accurate?" What this will accomplish is confirm that this is the primary concern, or else it will draw out what that concern really is. Either way, you've clarified in both your mind and the prospect's mind that this is a reluctance that must be effectively dealt with.

I should point out, however, that some of the older sales books I read made this "convert the objection into a question" seem a bit simpler than it really is. It does call for some finesse on your part in how you formulate your question. Here's a bad example. The prospect says, "Your price is way out of the ball park." Your response, "So, what you're really asking then, Bill, is does our

Objections: Obstacles or Opportunities?

premium system merit the increased investment. Is that right?" Well, DUH! ... allow me to applaud your keen insight there, Sherlock. This response simply comes across as contrived and manipulative.

A better way of handling this would be, "Bill, it's certainly not unreasonable to question price, particularly in relation to what you're currently paying. I'm sure your company expects that of you. However, if price weren't such a critical issue, would there be anything else that would keep my proposal from being the best overall solution to your needs?"

What you would have accomplished in this example is actually our next step which is "Isolate." Now your objective is to quickly point out how your system, because of better reliability and higher productivity, actually saves them money over the duration of the lease. If your sales job routinely calls for you to sell a premium product to prospects accustomed to a lower-priced item, then you must build a convincing argument that clearly proves value over price.

One of the best comebacks I've heard from a salesperson that sold a premium-priced product (upon hearing "Your price is too high") was, "Ironically, Bill, that's one of the main reasons why people choose our brand." My point is that you have now redirected this back into a continuing discussion and a closable-sales situation if you've properly done your homework in analyzing this prospect's needs. Your skill in formulating your question would have accomplished this.

Step # 4 – Isolate (this is a very critical step!)

This step is important because it allows you to ascertain whether this is the only obstacle to seeking favorable consideration on your proposal and moving forward with your presentation. The critical wording of this isolate step will determine whether there is some other underlying objection that hasn't yet surfaced. This tactic is designed to either identify and overcome the objection, thereby setting the stage for a trial close, or else it should uncover the true objection.

Continuing with our example: "Bill, other than your concern about meeting your company's high-service standards at a favorable value, is there any other reason you'd be reluctant to consider this?"

Step # 5 – Answer the objection effectively (and *then* have the prospect affirm that you have).

This is where your preparation and anticipation of frequently encountered objections really pays off. In every selling scenario, you eventually develop a list of most commonly encountered objections. As you do, you formulate your responses to these and you continually tweak these responses until they become tried and proven in the field. Once you're confident that you've answered the objection to the customer's satisfaction, you affirm it by saying something like, "Bill, wouldn't you agree that this program really could provide you with the on-demand support you need at a fair price?" Another universal type response is, "Just so I don't make any erroneous assumptions here, Bill, does that fully answer your concerns about …?"

Sometimes your response may also involve the use of testimonial letters, customer lists, or other supporting sales visual aids. It could incorporate a video that with today's technology can be quickly delivered from devices like an iPhone™. Technophiles should have a field day coming up with visually engaging responses to routinely encountered objections. What a great opportunity to challenge your creativity here.

Step # 6 – Attempt a trial close (if the timing is appropriate).

The reason why I say "if the timing is appropriate" is because you obviously shouldn't attempt a trial close if the first words out of a prospect's mouth are objection(s). If, on the other hand, you are well into your "Conviction" phase of your presentation, then this would be a good time to attempt a trial close.

For example: "Bill, now that you've agreed that this service plan does deliver value to your company at the service level you demand, how soon would you like to get

Objections: Obstacles or Opportunities?

started?" This tactic is what we refer to as isolate, then culminate. As we'll discuss later in the chapter on Closing, once you ask a closing question, SHUT UP! Do not say anything further until the customer gives their response. As you'll learn later in the chapter on Closing, if you give in to the urge to speak because the prospect is pausing too long, you negate this close attempt and have to try to work your way back into another one. In this instance, silence truly can be golden.

Let me also address the "stalls" scenario that this section identified. Stalls are a built-in defense mechanism we all have when we suddenly realize that a salesperson is on the verge of convincing us to make a buying decision right then. It's like a security breach in our self-control that elicits this automatic countermeasure. We're stalling for more time to reassure ourselves that this is absolutely a good decision to go ahead with.

By clearly understanding this rationalization process, professional salespeople are better able to facilitate a positive outcome for both parties. The salesperson must continue to provide reassurance so that the prospect feels fully confident that he's making a sound buying decision.

Stalls are oftentimes referred to as "smoke screens" because they frequently mask the real objection. In most cases, you can still use the same objection-handling strategy for stalls that you do for bonafide objections. The "Feel–Felt–Found" formula can oftentimes be used for maneuvering yourself into a sales dialogue. In other instances, the Stun Statement may be more effective.

Using the earlier stall example of, "I couldn't possibly consider such a proposal until after our budget is finalized," I suggest saying, "That's exactly why I'm here." As it's so aptly designed to do, this stun statement temporarily disables the prospect's defenses so you can launch your sales dialogue. I would continue with, "Like your company, many of my current customers had to investigate and evaluate the merits of a new program long before budgets were finalized. In doing so, you've demonstrated to your management that you're constantly exploring new ways to improve the company's bottom line. Now, I certainly don't want to presume to know what all your needs and concerns might be regarding a program like this, so how about if you tell me what's important to you?"

"Blitzing" – How to sack a recurring tough objection

Please indulge me for continuing to use examples from my Yellow Pages experience, but that's where many of my ideas were incubated. I also think they illustrate concepts that are easily transferrable to a variety of selling situations. If you're a football fan, then you certainly understand how blitzing works to try to undermine a strong passing game. In sales, blitzing is a preemptive strike designed to neutralize a tough objection by acknowledging its validity to the prospect *up front* and then showing how your product or service actually supports their position.

Fundamentals of Selling

My best example of this is from those Yellow Pages prospects/customers who immediately greeted me with "I get most of my customers from word-of-mouth advertising. I don't need anything in the Yellow Pages but my business name, address, and phone number." In my early Yellow Pages days, this was a tough one to counter because to take issue with it meant I was insulting the prospect's opinion, reputation, or advertising savvy.

My first sales manager taught me how to use the blitzing technique. On virtually every sales call where the advertiser had a long history of just maintaining minimal presence in their Yellow Pages directory, I used this approach. "Mrs. Smith, I bet you get the bulk of your customers through word-of-mouth advertising, right?" Note the important approach criteria that it did not easily lend itself to a response of "I wouldn't be interested." Rarely did I have anyone say no to this question. Their affirmation of my question set the stage for me to follow up with this. "Did you know that your competitors can actually steal some of these word-of-mouth referrals at

Objections: Obstacles or Opportunities?

the critical moment when they're ready to do business with you? Let me show you what I mean (while opening up the Yellow Pages to their primary classification)."

"Most of your satisfied customers who refer their friends to you don't always do so at the precise moment when your product or service is needed. Also, they don't generally recite your phone number or exact address. Consequently, at the critical moment when your word-of-mouth referral is ready to buy, they typically go to the Yellow Pages to look you up. Then what happens? A competitor's larger display ad grabs their attention while they're looking for your listing."

"For example, this ad here (as I illustrate in the phone book) says they offer 24-hour emergency service and accept all major credit cards. This could be just the key selling points that persuade *your* referral to call your competitor and not you. So, as I said, your competition succeeded in stealing one of your referrals. Why not invest in an insurance policy to protect your interests? As an added bonus, you'll also pick up a certain number of uncommitted Yellow Page shoppers who respond to the information that your ad provides to them."

At this point, I would typically show the prospect an idea for a display ad that I had drawn up in advance. This blitzing strategy did not contradict my prospect's position; it complemented and reinforced it.

Now, I'll admit that internet access has virtually made print Yellow Page advertising obsolete; however, this blitzing concept is still relevant and transferrable to any selling situation. Here are some other examples of blitzing commonly encountered objections:

- *Many of the companies I call on like yours have some concerns about the ability of a small manufacturing firm like us being able to compete effectively with the big guys. How do you feel about that?*
- *One of the things I hear most when I first approach*

Objections: Obstacles or Opportunities?

a company is "If it ain't broke, don't fix it." Can I offer you just one quick but important contradiction to that philosophy?

NOTE: Both of the above examples lend themselves well to the "backup supplier" sales strategy. It, in effect, asks the prospect, "Why not test drive our capability with no risk? After all, your best supplier was at one time unknown to you. Stuff happens, it's often said. You never know when one of your best and most reliable suppliers is going to fumble the ball, possibly for reasons outside their control. It's always a good idea to have a contingency backup plan in place."

- *A major obstacle for many companies who wish to consider upgrading their phone system is that they're locked into a long-term lease. Have you found this to be the case?*

My recommended strategy on this one is to have a lease buyout option available that allows you to blend this cost into the new, upgraded system lease or purchase.

Occasionally you may encounter prospects/customers who voice no objections all the way up to when you feel it's time to initiate your closing phase. It's always prudent in such cases to take the prospect's temperature, so to speak, by asking, "Based on what you've heard so far, do you have any concerns or see any drawbacks to this concept?" This is designed to ferret out any, as yet, undisclosed objections or concerns and thereby set the stage to begin your closing attempt(s). If you omit this step, you are more likely to encounter a stall from the prospect with them saying something like, "I'm just not sure, so I really would like more time to think it over." If you get this response, you employ the "I'd like to think it over" countermeasures discussed in the chapter on Closing.

As you can see, some creative thinking is called for here. Brainstorm your commonly encountered objections with your associates at your sales meetings. Operate like a NASCAR pit crew and continue to tweak your sales setup on these until you find your optimum performance settings. Comprehensive preparation in anticipating, cataloging, and perfecting effective responses to frequently encountered objections must be a top priority for you at all times. In this way, objections can become guideposts to opportunity, rather than obstacles to success.

Hostile Encounters & "Disarming" Techniques

In the normal course of selling, you will inevitably experience some hostile prospect and customer encounters from time to time. It's a normal part of the sales job. These challenges to your patience and professional skill can occur at any time. Consequently, there are specialized techniques called for in such situations that differ from the conventional objection-handling tactics just discussed. Recognizing this, you should try to gain an understanding of the underlying psychology from the prospect's perspective.

First of all, don't interpret this as an attack on you

personally. Usually the prospect is upset with circumstances and/or events that probably have nothing whatsoever to do with you. You just happen to be on the receiving end of his anger or frustration. It's up to you as a professional salesperson to try to defuse the situation. How do you do this?

The technique of disarming requires that you avoid creating an adversarial confrontation by not being judgmental in your response. Rather than being challenging in nature, your response is conciliatory. You attempt to initiate a neutral atmosphere that is conducive to understanding and resolving the prospect's hostility. Your carefully formulated response can quickly lower the prospect's anger and set the stage for peaceful negotiations. It begins with you acknowledging the prospect's right to be angry. Here's an example:

Customer: "You guys fumbled the ball one too many times last year, so now I'm cancelling my contract with you."

Objections: Obstacles or Opportunities?

Your response: "I can see you're very upset about this and understandably so. I'm frankly embarrassed by our shortcomings." (Pause for prospect's response.) "I'd really consider it a big favor if you'd be willing to share with me the details of how this all transpired."

Sales reps that are unskilled in disarming techniques have a tendency to get defensive in such situations. In the above scenario, they'd probably say something like, "Well, Bill, since I wasn't your account rep at the time, I really don't deserve the blame for that, do I?" Although this response may be factually accurate, it certainly doesn't acknowledge the customer's right to be angry, nor does it create a favorable setting for resolving the complaint. A little bit of humility can go a long way in diminishing the customer's hostility.

In most of the steps of *The Sales Track* reviewed thus far, I've repeatedly stressed the importance of you understanding the underlying psychology from the customer/prospect's perspective. In this situation, however, it's equally important that your demeanor convey to the customer where you're coming from psychologically. Disarming most effectively occurs as a result of the prospect interpreting your actions as conciliatory in nature. Another example of a situation that lends itself to a disarming response would be:

Prospect: "You guys never seem to understand that constantly expanding your product line is actually creating as many problems for me as opportunities."

Your response: "You know, Bill, I've never really thought of it in quite that way until I heard it from your perspective. Would you mind elaborating on that so I can see if there's a solution that better supports your needs."

Occasionally a customer or prospect's frustration may have been simmering a long time, and they've just been waiting for you to show up. This situation calls for exceptional control and understanding on your part. Remember that important guideline, "If you lose your cool, you no longer rule!" That's not to say you have to withstand verbal or physical abuse from a customer. In such

Objections: Obstacles or Opportunities?

instances, a tactfully executed retreat is probably the better part of valor. You can then attempt to regroup later, if appropriate.

You never want to contaminate the well, so to speak, by engaging in a game of blame and further alienating a good prospect or customer. Doing so pretty much closes the door to this account for any future opportunities. Most hostile or irate customers will gradually cool down on their own if you just allow them to vent their anger uninterrupted. The best way to turn this around and keep yourself in the game is to develop and constantly refine your disarming techniques. I urge you to use the skills development exercise in this chapter to begin building and enhancing your repertoire of disarming responses that are relevant to your occasional hostile encounters. The dividends will be well worth the investment of time and effort.

Another generic response that you can tweak to suit your particular selling circumstances would be as follows. This response will usually work to defuse an irate customer or prospect regardless of the exact nature of their grievance.

"Bill, my only objective at this point is to try to resolve this problem. I can understand if you feel we don't deserve the opportunity, but I hope you'll grant me just a few minutes. I'm sure that if one of your sales reps called on a long-standing loyal customer (or prospect) and encountered a similar situation, you would want your rep to at least try to understand how the problem occurred from the customer's point of view, wouldn't you? I may not be able to fully reconcile the issue to your complete satisfaction, but I owe it to you and to my employer to at least try. For me to withdraw from the situation without even offering to make amends is almost as bad as us committing the error in the first place. Would you be willing to elaborate on the problem to see if we can arrive at a resolution that's acceptable to you? I'd really consider it a big favor."

In some of these cases, you may later discover that the customer had partial or even complete responsibility for

Objections: Obstacles or Opportunities?

creating the problem. Regardless of that, just remember that your consolation prize for acquiescing was that you earned the chance to retain the customer's business or make a new sale. A buyer I used to call on regularly had a sign on the wall behind his desk. It read, "Fix the problem, not the blame." I've never forgotten that sound sales advice.

Fix the problem, not the blame!

Pause for the Skills Development Exercise on the next page.

Skills Development Exercise

Design some disarming statements that you can employ in the hostile or irate customer/prospect encounters you occasionally experience.

Chapter 7

Closing the Sale

Closing is to sales what scoring a touchdown is to football. You can engineer a beautifully executed drive down the field, but if you can't punch the ball over the goal line, you walk away empty handed. So it is with selling as well. Closing the sale is quite simply *the moment of truth*. As my variation on Thomas Macaulay's quote stated earlier, "The object of oratory is not just to educate, but to persuade."

With proper training, knowing how and when to close will become instinctive to you. This is certainly bolstered by you developing an attitude that you are helping facilitate a decision that the prospect will feel good about

Fundamentals of Selling

(remember my Datsun 300ZX story). The easier you make it for the prospect to buy, the more proficient you'll become at closing. That's where skilled technique becomes the difference maker in those who can effectively close and those who can't.

Most effective closes, in my opinion, subjugate the oftentimes anxiety-producing moment of decision to a secondary action that signals tacit approval. For example, the most effective closing technique I learned as a Yellow Pages sales rep was known as "closing on the copy sheet."[6] My first sales manager taught me this, and it became my bread-and-butter close. All Yellow Pages sales reps were required to prepare a "spec" (speculative) ad to take in with them on every sales call. A spec ad was simply an idea you prepared yourself or you had the in-house artist draw up for you. In your particular industry, think of it as the promotional piece on the item you're trying to sell.

---

[6] The "Copy Sheet" was the 8.5" x 11" document that every Yellow Page ad (both "spec" and existing) was individually displayed on, and the customer/prospect had to sign to approve the ad's layout. Copy sheets were addendums to the customer's Yellow Pages contract. The contract was the primary document that itemized each customer's entire advertising program by ad type and price.

Closing the Sale

You'll recall my earlier story of the Tampa furniture store where I inserted a photo of their new storefront in a larger display ad for my spec idea. Presenting this spec ad initiated my closing strategy while engaging the customer in its successful execution. Since this occurred very early in my presentation, I was also addressing the create interest, build desire and conviction, and handle objections right out of the box. I would ask questions about what the customer thought of the new (larger) layout and design.

Of course, it was not uncommon for some people to respond to my spec ad by saying that they just wanted to renew the same (smaller) ad they already had in the Yellow Pages. My response to this was to tell them that I felt like I would be short changing them if I didn't at least have some new ideas to show them to help increase their business or improve their existing advertising program.

I would then ask if they saw anything in the larger ad that they might like to incorporate into their existing ad while

I continued to focus on the new spec ad layout. I would also try to offer ideas on how they could better synchronize their Yellow Pages advertising with their other advertising, such as radio or newspaper, to reinforce their collective effectiveness (consultative selling). All the while, I would be giving supporting reasons for upgrading to the new, larger ad and how it could increase their business or help them attract a certain type of customer they wanted to increase their traffic on, etc.

Remember that properly diagnosing arms you with the selling points that build desire and solidify conviction. The customer's responses to my diagnosing questions allowed me to make on-the-spot changes to the spec ad layout as the customer looked on. When I felt like I had moved them to an adequate level of desire and conviction for this improved ad, I would say something like, "I'm going to need a good, sharp example of your new logo for our finished art. Do you have one I can take with me?"

When they proceeded to get me a copy of their logo, I

knew they had given (tacit) approval to the new, larger display ad. This "action" close on the copy sheet subjugated a direct "will you buy this ad" decision to an indirect means of securing their approval.

In some instances, this technique revealed tacit approval in other ways. For example, the customer might tell me to change sometime about the spec ad layout or add a graphic such as the brand-name logo(s) of products they carried. This, in essence, indicated that they had already bought the new ad in their mind.

Can this technique work for your particular product or service? In most cases, this concept is transferrable, as illustrated in the following examples:

- Installation of computer equipment involving multiple sites: "I'll need a list of your company sites involved, including the name and contact info of the person in charge at each site. Do you have one handy?"

- Business telephone system: While reviewing the list of optional features that can be programmed into the phone system, you ask the prospect to check off and initial which ones they want programmed into their system.

- Life insurance policy: "You would be entitled to a veteran's discount on premiums. Do you have a copy of your military Form DD–214 that I can get from you?"

- Certificate of *whatever*: If your completed sales paperwork typically involves having to include a copy of any kind of certificate, e.g., business license, proof of insurance, government certification, etc., use this as your action close item. "Do you have a copy of your business license I can get from you today?"

- Any consumer product or service that offers automatic bank draft payment plan: "I'm going to need a blank voided check from you for our automatic bank draft plan, which entitles you to 3 percent additional discount on your monthly premium. Do you have one handy?"

Closely associated with the action close is the "minor point" or "subordinate point" close. You simply substitute the prospect's response to a question regarding a minor point in place of them actually taking some physical action. Their response to your question can then indicate tacit approval of your proposal. Here are some examples.

- Realtor: Uses an illustration of the home's lot survey showing dimensions and property lines to ask the prospect where they thought a pool would work best on this lot.

- Incentive gift selection: If your company offers an incentive gift to purchasers, you simply show the prospect the promotional literature that illustrates their choices and ask them which one they would prefer.

- Scheduling calendar: If your sale involves an

installation, you pull out your calendar and ask the prospect what time frame would work best for them.

Pause for the Skills Development Exercise on the next page.

Skills Development Exercise

Design several action closes that are relevant to your particular product or service.

The previous action and minor point close examples should give you a good idea of how this concept works. These closing techniques have universal application to all types of products and services. The key to their effectiveness is that they subjugate the act of verbally acknowledging that they have bought to a subordinate act or response that signals they have made the buying decision in their mind.

Professional salespeople must develop an instinct that alerts them when it's time to begin the closing process. One technique for initiating this is to attempt a trial close. The trial close can be an action or minor point close, such as just discussed, or it can be very direct. Here's a direct one that has universal application.

"Bill, is there anything about what we just discussed that you feel you need to deliberate on any further?" If Bill says no, you can then close on a minor point such as, "Would next Thursday be a good date to take your first shipment?"

Closing the Sale

There's also the "alternate of choice" close, such as, "Would you prefer that in the navy or the red?"

If, on the other hand, Bill says he needs to deliberate on something, you have an objection that needs to be overcome and then you can attempt another trial close. Once you gain affirmation that you've handled that objection satisfactorily, you then say, "Bill, now that we've got that clarified, is there any other reason we shouldn't get this system installation scheduled right away?"

There's another closing technique that I suggest you use judiciously because it can come across as being somewhat manipulative. It's called the "sharp angle" or "return serve" close attempt. Here's an example.

A prospect for a new car has been giving off positive buying signals about a silver four-door luxury sedan. He asks the salesman if it comes with a GPS navigation system. The salesman could say that it is optional on that particular car, however, this would have simply answered the question without initiating the closing process. Sharp angling would use this response, "Would you buy the car today if I can get it with the GPS system?"

Here's another example. Your prospect says, "We would absolutely have to have online tech support 24/7." Your return serve trial close could be: "If we can guarantee to provide this, would we be able to go ahead and schedule your system survey right away?" Again, I suggest you use this technique carefully because it can come across as very abrupt and some people will recoil at this tactic. A careful choice of words, however, can make the "return serve" close an effective tool in your arsenal.

Somewhat similar in its concept and execution is the concession close. This can be used when you sense that your prospect is teetering on the brink of a favorable decision and just needs a little incentive to push him or her over the edge. In its simplest form, a concession close would be along the following lines:

"If I can get my sales manager to agree to that price, are you prepared to go ahead with this today?" I recommend that you have at least a couple of default concession closes in your arsenal that can be used on your typical sales calls.

Pause for the Skills Development Exercise on the next page.

Skills Development Exercise

List some typical (closing phase) questions you occasionally get from prospects and devise "return serve" closing responses for each.

Devise three concession closes that are relevant to your standard selling situation.

Closing the Sale

You should recognize that it's normal to encounter some buyer resistance during the closing phase. After all, prospects obviously realize they're on the brink of making a buying decision and most often, they just need added reassurance. In some cases, they may want to stall for additional time to think it over.

We might as well address the pesky "I'd like to think it over" right now since it's encountered in all fields of selling. From the salesperson's perspective, it's important to realize that you must calmly and confidently persevere and try to maintain your momentum while you're this close to concluding a sale. If you have to make a callback, you'll essentially be starting the sales process all over again. As professional salespeople, we need to understand that this phenomenon is just an innate defense mechanism that everyone has to making buying decisions. This is where the "facilitator" role is the key to overcoming this obstacle.

In the chapter on Presenting with Benefits, I said that to facilitate is to make easier or more convenient. That's what you must do here. The prospect needs for you to help them feel that this is a good buying decision for them to act favorably on *now*. Oftentimes, this reaction is due to apprehension over making that large of an unplanned expenditure. Therefore, it's essentially a value equation.

Have you adequately convinced the prospect that the value (benefits derived) clearly outweigh the cost? I can tell you that numerous sales books advocate exerting the full-court press when confronted with the "I'd like to think it over" stall. They suggest using a comeback along the lines of, "I certainly agree that it's important to thoroughly think this over. What exactly is it that you'd like to think over?"

I frankly prefer incorporating a bit more finesse in your response so that it comes across as less confrontational. One technique is to employ the "criteria" close attempt. In this close, you respond to "I'd like to think it over" with something along these lines.

Closing the Sale

"Ann, I can certainly appreciate you wanting to give this careful consideration, and you're right in doing so. It's been my experience that the people who ultimately decide to go with our program do so for one or more of the following three reasons: (then articulate your best three reasons for buying, and as you do, ask the prospect if she agrees that's important to her)."

At the conclusion of this, you say something like, "I'm sure this decision may seem a bit overwhelming for you, but right now, at this particular moment, you're in the best position to make a well-informed decision. By making it now, all the relevant facts and important details are still clear and fresh in your mind. Wouldn't you agree that moving ahead on this project now would allow you to start enjoying the benefits of _____ immediately and thereby turn your attention to other important business matters?"

At this point, **shut up** and wait for the prospect to respond. Even if the prospect's response is slow in coming and the silence is deafening, wait for their response. If you speak before getting their response, you've relinquished your closing opportunity.

Another variation of the criteria close is based on the old "Ben Franklin Balance Sheet close." This is where you would tell prospects about how Ben Franklin used to carefully evaluate tough decisions by drawing up a list of the pros and cons regarding that decision. I used a modified version of this tactic by carrying a predesigned document that already listed eight or ten of the primary reasons why most prospects went with my product/service. These positive buying reasons would be listed on the "Pro" designated left side of the page with a dividing line running vertically down the center of the page. A "Con" heading would then be shown on the right side of the page. So as not to appear totally biased, I even listed several potential drawbacks that I occasionally encountered, such as price or my company's size. These were drawbacks that I felt confident I could address and overcome if I hadn't already done so earlier in my presentation.

Closing the Sale

This buying validation document can oftentimes provide just the right amount of added reassurance needed to close the sale. Your close would usually be consummated via a direct close question such as, "Is there really any reason why we shouldn't go ahead and get this installation scheduled right away?" This document then becomes a good leave-behind piece to help reinforce the decision in the buyer's mind afterward.

Pause for the Skills Development Exercise on the next page.

Skills Development Exercise

Design a "criteria" close relevant to your particular product or service.

Design a "Ben Franklin Balance Sheet" document that highlights the "Pro" features/benefits of your particular product or service. Also, identify three items to list on the "Con" side that are easy to overcome.

Closing the Sale

Another effective tactic can be a final appeal to the prospect's good nature where you say something like: "Bill, do we really need to go into overtime on this? You've already devoted a lot of time reviewing proposals and talking to prospective vendors about this. You've agreed that my proposal definitely meets your needs and is very competitive. The other critical ingredient here is that you also get me as your dedicated account manager. I will be here throughout the installation process to ensure that everything goes smoothly as promised. I'll continue to provide any needed support and backup throughout our partnership. Is there really any reason to delay taking advantage of these benefits today?"

You can sometimes lessen the likelihood of the dreaded stall by employing some preemptive questions during your diagnosing phase. For example, you could say, "Just to be sure I'm working within your time frame, how soon do you hope to make a decision on this?" You might also ask, "Will there be anyone else other than yourself who needs to be involved in this decision?" This can certainly help reinforce your attempts to push for a conclusion when confronted with a stall.

Sometimes, even with our best efforts, a prospect simply won't be pushed into making a decision right then. In such cases, if you absolutely have to make a callback, set up a date and time for the callback and make it clear that you'd appreciate a definite decision one way or the other at that time.

I would also try to preempt my competition from getting the sale by asking the prospect if they did decide to go with some other company, would they at least give me the opportunity to meet or beat that proposal before they signed?

An effective reinforcing tool here is a well designed vendor qualifications checklist that you leave with the prospect to compare each candidate. If you don't try to establish these conditions up front, it can become the never-ending callback scenario and your chances of

Closing the Sale

successfully closing that sale diminish with each successive return visit.

You should also have some new ideas to launch your callback presentation with to try to regenerate that buying excitement. Opening with a new testimonial letter or validation trade magazine article about your product or service helps you regain momentum.

If you're greeted with, "We've decided to go with someone else," you can try to regain a foothold using the backdoor approach. This is where you thank them for their time and consideration and then simply ask them what the deciding factor in their decision was. I always used my "help me out" appeal by saying, "You could really do me and my company a big favor if you could help us better understand where we're falling short." This can present you with an opening to renegotiate with them if they haven't already signed a contract. If they have, you didn't do a very good job in asking them beforehand to give you a chance to meet or beat any deal before they committed to it.

Pause for the Skills Development Exercise on the next page.

Skills Development Exercise

Design a standard Vendor Qualifications Checklist that you can use as a leave-behind document when you're unable to overcome the "I'd like to think it over" stall.

Closing is the successful culmination of an effective sales presentation. It takes practice and continuous effort to improve your technique. You'll probably find, like most salespeople, that you develop some signature closes of your own that become your trademark closes. I believe that the key to success is that you feel comfortable and confident in the ones you use. It's an indispensable skill if you are to succeed in sales.

The skills development exercises for this chapter should help you in defining or refining your game-winning style. In those cases where your best efforts fail to close the sale, your exit should be done in such a way that it leaves the door open to revisit that opportunity at some later date. You never know what might happen in the meantime. The winning vendor might fumble the ball or fail to deliver as promised, and you may be right back in the ball game. Always exit graciously, professionally, and express genuine gratitude for the prospect's consideration.

**Exhilaration rarely comes from
doing things that are easy.**

NOTES

SalesCadre.com

Go For It!

Chapter 8

Game Winning Plays

There are a lot of parallels in what contributes to success in both sales and sports. It's a proven fact that the outcome of most football games boils down to several critical game changing plays that ultimately result in victory for the team that effectively executes them. Along similar lines, I've listed some game winning sales plays below that can help you win more sales.

Don't wear out your welcome – If your strategy for capturing a new account typically requires multiple attempts before you succeed, it's important that you vary your presentation each time to keep it fresh and interesting. Try to provide some new insights and ideas each visit that can regenerate that spark of interest or curiosity.

Perseverance is best fueled by innovative approaches that rejuvenate the prospect's enthusiasm as well as your own. Bring in a new video clip, a testimonial letter, a validation article from a trade publication, etc. Make each callback meaningful and inspiring to the prospect if you want to sustain your sales momentum.

Consultative selling vs. Transactional selling – Transactional selling is simply focusing on successfully concluding the sales transaction with minimal effort. In its purest sense, a person selling newspapers on the street corner would be engaging in transactional selling. To elevate this a notch or two, a door-to-door salesperson selling office cleaning services to businesses is also engaging in transactional selling.

Consultative selling, on the other hand, expands the process from just trying to conclude the sales transaction to educating the prospect and possibly helping to solve peripheral problems as part of your overall sales effort. For example, when I once sold traffic warning signs to electric utilities, I differentiated myself from my competition by becoming an expert on the Department of Transportation regulations that governed the use of such signs. In doing so, I was able to educate my prospects and customers about the importance of their company complying with these regulations.

I also developed a pocket guidebook for their utility crews that explained the various circumstances under which they were required to deploy these traffic warning signs when they were working on or near public roadways. This guidebook became a free resource that my company provided whenever a utility purchased our products.

We also did field training for their crews. I once helped another utility design a compact sign storage system for their trucks to store their signs and the stands that the signs mounted on. In addition, I worked with this utility's training department to develop a training video on traffic safety for their linemen. My efforts helped solidify my position as a favored supplier with this utility. Such actions above and beyond just trying to conclude a sale can elevate you to a consultant's status rather than just another vendor vying for a company's business.

The pre-call psyche-up ritual – Whenever I'm about to give an especially important presentation, I go through a pre-call psyche-up ritual. For you younger folks, that would be known as "getting stoked." It's a visualization process that's similar to what professional athletes use. The routine I devised is what I call "conjuring up my cheerleading squad." I imagine that about a dozen or so of the people whose respect and approval I've most valued throughout my life are seated together in the observation balcony of a hospital operating room. You know, like on the TV show *Grey's Anatomy*. They are collectively seated up there about to observe my presentation and cheer me on. Consequently, I psyche myself into delivering my absolute best performance in front of this cherished group because their opinion is so highly esteemed to me. Try it yourself and I think you'll experience how it can truly elevate your performance level.

Leverage your cyberpower – The Internet has provided you with a tremendous tool for enhancing your sales efforts. You can instantly deliver video content to your prospect/customer on an iPhone™ or similar device. You can embed YouTube videos into your personal sales blog or e-mail links to such videos to your prospects. It's now quick and easy to make your own videos and e-mail them to a prospect. You can research articles on topics you've determined would be relevant or of interest to your prospect and e-mail them as a follow-up (remember consultative selling). Information can be packaged, showcased, and delivered in a variety of formats today. Separate yourself from the herd of other competitors by being innovative.

Casting a lure at trade shows – Industry trade shows are a great source of leads for most companies. However, the irony of these staged sales extravaganzas is that even though most attendees are probably there to investigate new products and services, many of them are still hesitant to engage vendors in conversation. I suspect it goes back to that innate buyer's resistance to putting oneself into a sales situation where you feel someone is going to try to persuade you to make a buying decision you may not feel prepared to make at the moment. Consequently, this scenario calls for a low-pressure approach that will lure a prospect into a dialogue.

One of the best examples I can relate occurred to me at a home improvement show. I basically just went for some decorating ideas and something to do on a cold Sunday afternoon. As I was checking out the exhibits, a screen room manufacturer's display caught my attention. As a homeowner, I had often considered adding a screen room to my back porch area to provide me with a nice outdoor leisure room, but I never seriously pursued it.

A salesman who noticed me checking out their display from the aisleway walked over and said, "Relaxing in your own private bug-free shady sanctuary sounds pretty appealing, doesn't it?"

As a sales trainer, I thought to myself what a great low-key, no-pressure approach he just made. That mind-opening question resulted in him engaging me in a sales dialogue where he skillfully began his diagnosing. What he learned was that my house was currently for sale, and as a consequence, I wasn't really a viable prospect. However, I still had to admire the finesse of his approach. I suspect it probably did work on some other attendees that weekend that didn't have their homes on the market and were lured into a sales dialogue with this skillfully executed approach.

Regardless of your product or service, the lesson here is the same. It's possible to design your opening remarks in such a way that they invite the prospect to engage you in an exploratory sales dialogue. This technique works equally well with a retail selling environment such as an electronics store. If your sales department is wide-screen TVs, you should always greet browsers with a smile and an introduction such as, "Hi, I'm Jim. Just let me know if I can help." Then, if you notice that they are spending some time carefully scrutinizing the various models, casually work your way over to them with something in your hand like a clipboard. The clipboard allows you to have copies of important sales visuals readily at hand, such as extended warranty information, no interest financing details, free delivery incentives, validation articles, etc. It also allows you to appear as though you're just going about your normal sales associate duties such as inventorying the display models.

When an opening presents itself, say something like, "You know this Panasonic Slim Line plasma was rated tops in its class by *Consumer Reports*.[7] Here's a copy of *Consumer Reports'* latest ratings on HDTVs." (***Pause***—Remember, visual aids help to engage prospects.)

"What are some of the features you're looking for in a HDTV?" Such a low-key sales approach with a prospect generally invites engagement that can reveal clues to what buying motives would lead to a purchase. Most retail prospects would be receptive to this type of low-

---

[7] Such product-related claims should, of course, be accurate and certifiable.

pressure, helpful sales approach.

Post sales call habits – You should get in the habit of taking some time to record your evaluation and afterthoughts about the call you just concluded. Use the "Sales Call Evaluation" form in this manual to note this information. This can definitely be very helpful if you have to make a follow-up call to finalize the sale. It can also serve to catalog those recurring objections and obstacles for which you ultimately want to devise effective countermeasures.

Take the chill out of cold calling – In most cases, some amount of prospecting is still an indispensable part of selling. It just comes with the territory. On a regular basis you have to plant your soles on the sidewalk and make some cold calls. I prefer to think of them (and refer to them), however, as *opportunity* calls. It's incumbent upon sales trainers and managers to impart this attitude to our salespeople about these types of calls.

If your line of sales involves calling on businesses, it's

almost as if corporate America has devised a screening process whereby only the most creative and resourceful salespeople ever succeed in penetrating their barriers. In the majority of cases, you'll probably only be able to extract a person's name and possibly their direct phone number when making an opportunity call.

Since so many corporate offices today only grant access to someone with a preset appointment, I've often just sat in my car in the parking lot until I saw an employee arriving or departing. I then went up to that individual and inquired about who they would suggest I call regarding my product. Armed with this information, you'll need to employ the telephone prospecting techniques discussed in Chapter Three on "The Approach." These security measures have just about relegated traditional in person opportunity calling obsolete.

You can still make some effort, however, as you're driving from one appointment to your next. If you spot a potential prospect along your route and have enough time to make a quick stop, then it can be a worthwhile endeavor.

Game Winning Plays

Basically, it's just intelligence gathering to help qualify that company as a viable prospect. It also affords you the opportunity to try different approaches to penetrating the screening process.

You may still occasionally encounter the "gatekeeper" secretary whose mission it is to prescreen salespeople. Their standard question is, "May I ask what this is regarding?" You may recall that this topic was discussed earlier in the book in the section regarding the Telephone Approach. Once again, an effective strategy is to devise a response that the secretary typically wouldn't feel knowledgeable enough to handle. For example, if you're selling computer software, your response might be along these lines, "Yes, do you know if your IT system is presently receiving updates under the new Quasar protocol?" This tactic generally causes her to defer to whoever in the company would be the most appropriate individual for you to try to gain an appointment with. What it avoids is the secretary unilaterally determining that they wouldn't be interested.

Recognize that a certain amount of prospecting is essential to generating sales. View each opportunity call as an accrual toward making a sale. It's a numbers game. The more opportunity calls you make (by phone or in person), the closer you get to making another sale.

The well designed leave-behind piece – To follow up on the opportunity calling paragraph above, you need to design a leave-behind piece of information that you attach your business card to. Ideally, it should be one page only and something other than your standard product/service brochure. It must be worded in such as way as to spark interest or arouse curiosity and thus generate a return phone call or e-mail. It has the same requirement as making a prospecting phone call. You're simply trying to secure an appointment, not make a sale. Therefore, the information piece that you leave behind must be compelling in its message.

As an example, the headline of an information piece might read, "A recent FTC ruling has significantly affected virtually every business in your industry. Are you fully briefed on how this could potentially impact your operations?" (*Business Week* – January 18, 2010.) The information could go on to say, "Our five-minute survey can determine if your company is in full compliance under this new ruling." It could also show a small excerpt from the actual magazine article and give the URL address to the full article on the internet. You conclude by saying, "Please give me a call or send me an e-mail to discuss how we can help."

NOTE: The above referenced *Business Week* article is for illustration purposes only and is not an actual article that appeared in *Business Week*. This tactic is known as validation selling because you incorporate a third party, such as a trade or news publication, to validate and lend credibility to your claim. Be constantly vigilant for news or magazine articles that can support your consultative efforts at securing new customers. You'll recall how the Tampa newspaper article worked to break down the barrier for me when I was selling business telephone systems. Such validation articles can definitely be effective door openers for you.

Get over it and move on! As professional salespeople, we must recognize and accept the fact that a certain percentage of people you call on are going to be totally unreceptive and occasionally downright rude. Don't dwell too much on this because in all probability it's not personal. It happens to even the most seasoned sales professionals. Be polite and don't lose your composure. Thank them for their time and move on to the next prospect. You mustn't allow one person's closed-mindedness short-circuit your day.

I generally take a few minutes after such encounters to analyze how I might have modified my approach to improve the outcome. I then mentally catalog that idea so I can try my revised approach during my next similar situation. I'm reminded of a quote[8] by Dr. Stephen Covey in his book, *The 7 Habits of Highly Effective People* that I've modified slightly. My version of his quote is, "It's

---

[8] Dr. Covey's actual quote was, "It's not what happens to us, but our response to what happens to us that hurts us."

not what happens to us, but rather how we respond to what happens to us that ultimately determines how we will be affected."

One of my favorite analogies regarding objection to price – Sometimes injecting a bit of wit into your response can help ease the tension. One of my favorite analogies about my price being too high goes something like this. "In order for most companies to lower their price, it generally entails giving up something in terms of quality or service. For example, a great way to cut the cost of your health insurance premium in half is to convert to a policy that only provides coverage on the odd days of the month." This response is a universally applicable lead-in to explaining how value justifies price.

It's important to be personable – Don't overlook the importance of people skills when selling. Most prospective buyers like to feel as though they're viewed as human beings and not just a potential order. Engage them in conversations about themselves and show genuine interest in their responses. One way to do this is to ask them what some of the biggest challenges are that they face in their job. You can also ask them about their history with the company and who their major competitors are. You can sometimes leverage questions into revealing clues about how to sell that account.

For example, you can say something like, "I can only imagine that dealing with vendors on a day-to-day basis can be challenging. Can you offer any advice to someone like me who's just starting out?" People appreciate having their opinions valued.

On a more personal note, you can be observant of pictures, plaques, trophies, and other memorabilia displayed in their office that can trigger questions about their life outside the office. I once had to call on a buyer with a major telephone company who was about as forthcoming with information as a totem pole. When I noticed a picture of a 1957 Ford Thunderbird hanging on his wall, I asked him about it. That was the magic trigger that got him to talking and eventually he opened up about his needs relative to my product. Generally, when people go to the trouble to showcase a photograph in their office, it's a pretty safe bet that it has special meaning to them. You can employ this tactic by simply saying something like, "I hope you'll excuse me for getting off track momentarily, but that's a great looking photo." Such impromptu diversions can oftentimes be just the thing that breaks the stalemate and gets the prospect to open up with you. Think of it like this. Selling is not that different from the age-old courtship ritual in the following sense. You can come across as clever, but still not be likeable. It's important that you be personable. People are more inclined to buy from persons they like.

Make it fun! I always found it both enjoyable and effective to occasionally inject some fun in my approach. You'll recall the "It's Coming! Are You Ready?" buttons we had made up when I was selling telephone systems. Why not come up with your own button idea that could arouse curiosity and create a favorable atmosphere for you to engage the prospect in dialogue. How about one that reads, "Ask me why"; "I know a secret"; or "You

Fundamentals of Selling

don't want to miss out on this!" These buttons can be very effective dialogue starters in a retail sales environment.

I also like the idea of carrying one of the Staples "Easy" buttons in with you and setting it in front of a prospect when you say, "I promise to make this easy."

Or you could find a picture of someone dressed in a heavy parka with a fur-lined hood and snow boots standing in a frigid-looking snowy scene. Show this to the prospect who greets you with "I wouldn't be interested" and tell him that's your predecessor who got transferred to Minot, North Dakota, because he couldn't manage to introduce himself and his company to five new prospects a day.

When I sold flame-resistant work clothing, I had a doll clothes seamstress make me up some orange coveralls the size of a Ken doll. When I called on a new prospect, I pulled out my mini-coveralls and asked if he had heard about the extreme shrinkage that was commonplace on flame-resistant coveralls coming in from off-shore manufacturers. These fun tactics can create a light, non-aggressive approach that will oftentimes convince an unreceptive prospect to at least allow you to proceed a little further into your sales dialogue. Remember that sales axiom: "Selling is knowing what to say, how to say it, and when to say it."

Always leave 'em smiling – Whenever your approach attempt falls short or you fail to make the sale, always leave the prospect with a favorable impression of how you handled the situation. Thank them for their time and tell them that they've really helped you to better understand the challenges they're confronted with in their particular industry. Conclude by saying that if you can ever be of service to them that you hope they'll give you the opportunity to help. Circumstances can and do change and this prospect who wasn't interested today could be a receptive prospect at some later date.

Cataloging countermeasures – Effective salespeople must become highly adept at allaying fears in the prospect's mind. Some typical fears that are universal to all types of selling are: paying too much, purchasing too quickly, buying the wrong or inappropriate item, being among the first to try something new or different, etc. How do you develop this skill? You begin to mentally catalog those prospect fears that you routinely encounter and then devise effective strategies to counter them.

Hone your skills on low-probability prospects – Virtually every selling field has a certain percentage of prospects that are traditionally considered low potential. You can use these prospects as opportunities to practice and refine your selling skills. In my Yellow Pages sales days, examples of such accounts were "Financial Planners" or "Title Insurance Companies." These types of accounts typically didn't invest much, if any, of their advertising budget on Yellow Pages. Consequently, they were an ideal situation to try out new presentation ideas without risking or wasting much sales collateral.

Experiment with new creative approaches that you figure these prospects haven't seen before. These training calls can be especially productive when you're having a really successful sales week and want to leverage that enthusiasm into some new ideas.

The value of a pre-call – There's a saying in football that great defenses win championships. If your sales job entails having to renew contracts, agreements, policies, etc., on a scheduled interval, then a pre-call can be a prudent defensive tactic. This is especially true on your larger, key accounts.

Ideally, you should try to stop by unannounced. However, with security concerns being what they are today and preset appointments virtually a necessity, this may not always be possible. Be that as it may, on a pre-call, it's like you showing up unarmed, waving a white flag. You tell the customer that you just wanted to stop by and set an appointment for a full *review* of their contract (which you don't have the new copy of yet) and see how things are going. This then allows you to take the customer's temperature, so to speak, about the contract renewal and if they have any concerns, requests for changes, additions, etc. If they tell you that they intend to cancel, then you have virtual immunity to explore their issues without actually having to formally accept their cancellation (because you don't yet have their paperwork, remember?). As long as you don't get defensive but rather act conciliatory and understanding of their position, this buys you the time needed to go back and prepare your defense against this looming cancellation.

Of course, if the information gathered is positive, then you simply set the appointment to come back for an easy renewal or possibly an increase based on the information extracted during the pre-call.

By the way, don't squander the opportunity to solicit information from the receptionist or secretary if the owner or primary contact isn't in when you make your pre-call. If you treat them with courtesy and respect, they can usually be very forthcoming with details about the owner's intentions.

Capture your creative thoughts – Creative thoughts have a tendency to occur unexpectedly and at inconvenient times, such as when you're driving or trying to get to sleep. Because of the transient nature of such ideas, I suggest you devise a system for recording them immediately because they do tend to fade quickly. I recommend that you keep a digital tape recorder in your car or use the record function of your cell phone to capture the essence of the idea. You should also keep a small notebook or recorder on the nightstand next to your bed. Trust me when I tell you that these creative flashes are fleeting and probably won't be there the next day if you fail to record them the moment they're fresh.

Handling buyer hesitancy – It's not uncommon when prospective buyers find themselves on the brink of purchasing an unplanned impulse buy item such as a widescreen TV, surround sound stereo speaker system, new laptop computer, new furniture, etc.— to hesitate and balk at making a decision. In most cases, they're simply afraid of making a wrong decision and need reassurance.

An effective technique in such instances is to exert just a little subtle assertiveness by going for a direct close. Here's an example: "You know, Bill, I sense that you really want this pretty bad, right? I see this happen here everyday with other people, so I'll ask you the same thing I ask them.

"What's your biggest apprehension that could keep you from enjoying this well deserved reward right now?"

Another variation of this is, "You know, Bill, I sense that you still have some reservations about this purchase that haven't come out in the open yet. I'd really like a chance to see if it's something I can help resolve for you." This tactic will usually provide you with an objection that you can then deal with effectively, isolate, and close on.

If no objection is expressed, then the other alternative you're left with is to go for a minor point close. For example, "Shall I have it delivered or would you rather take it home with you today?"

NOTE: Many retail consumer items offer a time frame during which the buyer can return the item for a full refund. Use this added reassurance if necessary to get that item home and the enjoyment of it launched.

I bet you can appreciate where I'm coming from – If you're constantly competing with larger, more established firms and the business prospects you call on face a similar competitive challenge, try this statement as part of your appeal. "You know, Bill, I suspect that you occasionally encounter this yourself, having to go up against the big guys, right? Then you can probably appreciate where I'm coming from when I tell you that we can _____(review your competitive advantages)_____. Are these similar advantages that you promote when vying for new business?"

Credibility building via consultative selling – An excellent way to build credibility for yourself and your company is to provide tools to your prospects that help them make sound buying decisions. This tactic is especially effective with purchasing agents who have responsibility for multiple product and service lines.

Because of the breadth and diversity of the lines they procure, many purchasing agents are ill equipped to develop thorough and detailed "Request for Quotes"[9] (RFQs) on some of these items. Oftentimes this is due to the fact that they're new in the position and have limited experience with certain items they source. This affords you the opportunity to exploit that need by providing helpful guidance and essential input. This generally entails thoroughly analyzing all the variables regarding the design and performance requirements relative to that product or service. Then you develop and provide support tools such as a spreadsheet listing detailed specifications for the full scope of items that could potentially be requested.

An example from my consulting experience is when I developed a spreadsheet of generic design/performance specifications for flame-resistant (FR) work uniforms for

---

[9] Also referred to as "Request for Proposal" or RFP.

electric utility companies. This document was a tremendous time saver for the purchasing agents I provided it to because it was thorough, nonproprietary in nature, and editable to suit their particular needs. It also supported my clients' objectives by positioning them as the expert in the FR work apparel industry and a valuable resource to the prospect.

A companion document to this spreadsheet that I also developed was a guidebook on how to structure an effective RFQ for a flame-resistant clothing program. This was also very well received because it covered many aspects of a properly administered clothing program that numerous purchasing agents had never encountered but agreed were vitally important. Naturally this document emphasized all the strong points that my client brought to the table, but it also levied design and performance specs that made it very difficult for inferior vendors to meet all the requirements. This made it virtually impossible for bidders with low-quality products to steal the deal on low price alone.

This tactic can encompass other support tools such as training guides, white papers, comparison charts, reference files, etc. You may recall the work zone safety guidebook that I developed for Tampa Electric. This definitely positioned me as the expert with that company, and they became a loyal customer throughout my tenure with the supplier I represented.

I'm not proposing that you have to develop all these resources by yourself. It can be a collaborative effort with other members of your sales team or support staff. I strongly urge you to make this (peripheral problem) consultative tactic a key element of your sales arsenal.

When prospects seek several bids – When faced with a selling situation where your prospect desires several bids before making a decision, you can improve your chances for ultimately capturing that sale with the following preemptive appeal. When you drop off your quote to the buyer, set the stage with the following: "Bill, we obviously believe strongly that our system is the best one available on the market. I earn my living by convincing people like you that this is the case. Naturally if we found that more and more companies were opting for our competitor's product, we'd want to know how we could remedy our deficiency. I'd like to ask you a favor. If you ultimately decide not to go with our proposal, before you sign a contract, would you be willing to share with me the reason(s) that made the difference?" This strategy can afford you the opportunity to come back and possibly save the sale with the objection-handling techniques discussed in Chapter Six.

Last-minute salvage effort – When it appears that you've lost the deal to a competitor, try this last-minute tactic. "Mrs. Jones, I really appreciate the consideration you've shown me throughout this process. You've been very helpful and forthcoming in explaining your needs and requirements. May I ask you just one final question. Are you 100 percent certain that the proposal you're accepting fully meets all your needs and expectations, or is there any room for improvement before you commit?" This will frequently provide you with the information you need to try to resell your proposal, your company, and yourself as the best overall choice.

Putting price into a plausible perspective – One of the best techniques for overcoming the "too high" (or too much higher) price objection is to reduce the cost down to a per day perspective. If your price is $30 a month higher than the competitor your prospect is favoring, talk in terms of a dollar a day more to get better performance, quality, warranty, service, etc. If it's a discretionary purchase that's not really replacing an existing item (like a swimming pool), then again translate it into dollars per day or how many family meals out or movie tickets that would equate to. For business items, comparing the additional costs to projected savings realized through increased efficiency, greater productivity, less maintenance, longer service life, etc., is an effective strategy.

Be prudent with preliminary pleasantries – Earlier in this chapter, I stressed the need to be personable. However, it's also important to be prudent about your opening pleasantries. It's not uncommon for new, inexperienced salespeople to resort to pleasant chitchat in their opening. This is mainly due to nervousness and not yet being fully confident in one's skill level.

You should be prudent with this practice because it can undermine your chances to arouse interest in the prospect or customer. To some extent, I think this depends on whether you're calling on an established customer or a new prospect. An established customer may be more receptive to such preliminaries because they're expecting you to review their account and recommend enhancements. With a new prospect, however, you must arouse interest or curiosity quickly or you won't gain any sales traction. Although you may find a ten-minute story about your son's first Little League home run enchanting, you could lose your opportunity to stir the prospect's sales interest in the process.

On the other hand, some personality types actually enjoy some amount of personal banter in their dealings with salespeople. The key is really to determine at what stage of the sales presentation this is prudent. It's always best to take your cues from a person's body language. If it signals that the prospect is getting impatient, then you should quickly transition back into your sales presentation.

Frankly, I think such pleasantries are best suited to post-close conversation, while you're finishing up any associated paperwork. This provides a cordial distraction, thus, preventing your prospect from rehashing their decision too much during your wrap-up. In some cases, the roles may be reversed when your prospect wants to digress with personal stories of his own. For example, let's say that the prospect is the one relating a story of his son's latest proud moment. You can use a "bridge" like the following example to subtly redirect the prospect back into your sales presentation.

Your response to the prospect's story: "You know parenting demands much of the same discipline and skill as running a business, don't you agree? For example, you have to make tough choices that are in the best interests of the enterprise." You would then follow this up with a feature/benefit statement that is directly relevant to the prospect's needs. This maneuver allows you to regain control of the interview and maintain your sales momentum.

The simple power of a smile – Think about your own experiences. When you walk up to a fast-food counter and you're greeted warmly with a smile as opposed to a clerk whose facial expression and tone indicates that they hate their job, how does this impact your attitude about the service you're about to receive? Both a smile and a frown can be equally infectious. Always greet your prospects/customers with a smile and exit the same way.

NOTES

SalesCadre.com

Go For It!

Chapter 9

Staying on Track

Maintaining a positive mental attitude is essential to sustaining success in professional sales. It's not uncommon to experience occasional moments of self-doubt. That's quite normal. What's important is how you respond to these sinking spells. Dwelling on lost sales, setbacks, and other negative events can gradually build up like cholesterol and clog your mental arteries. As one of my favorite singer/songwriters, Jimmy Buffett, likes to say, you occasionally have to *mental floss.* Your creative talents will flourish best under a positive and optimistic attitude. Conversely, pessimism undermines your sales effectiveness and short circuits your creative energy. The best antidote for a negative attitude and associated feelings is a daily dose of positive thoughts and affirmations.

Just as it's important to develop a physical regimen for staying healthy, you should also have a mental health plan. The selling profession can be stressful at times and thus requires the use of some stress reducers. Your performance prescription should be tailored to what you respond to best. It could be listening to music, motivational tapes, reading, jogging, writing in your journal, posting to your blog or Facebook page, etc.

Regardless of what you include in your regimen, I think reading for enrichment and not just entertainment is a must. The great inspirational authors like Napoleon Hill, Dr. Norman Vincent Peale, Dale Carnegie, Dr. Wayne Dyer, Rev. Robert Schuller, Denis Waitley, Anthony Robbins, Dr. Stephen Covey, and others have had a positive influence on millions of readers over the years. The books by these great writers should be a part of your routine reading. Refer back to them from time to time and reread the paragraphs and sentences you have highlighted. Not only is this a great source of inspiration, it can also trigger creative ideas and solutions to problems you've been wrestling with. Sales education and self-improvement should be an ongoing and never-ending commitment.

One of the best ideas I ever received from a sales trainer was to develop my own "inspiration manual." An inspiration manual is essentially a scrapbook that chronicles your successes, goals, dreams, accomplishments, aspirations, etc. It serves as a constantly evolving reminder of what you can achieve if you set your mind to it and work hard toward it.

You can easily assemble an inspiration manual in a 3-ring binder. I prefer the kind with a clear cover that allows you to insert a photo or picture of some kind. I personally chose a beautiful tropical island scene with turquoise water and a white sandy beach. I found this picture in a travel magazine. It represents the ideal tropical escape for me.

For you, it could be a snowcapped mountain scene, a

trout stream, or hang gliding over a scenic valley. It could also be a photo of you accepting the class valedictorian award. The point is to make it personal to your particular dreams, successes, and desires.

The cornerstone elements of your manual should be mementos of your greatest achievements. These are the accomplishments of which you are most proud. In my case, successfully completing the rigorous 26-week infantry officer candidate school at Fort Benning, Georgia, and graduating as an Army second lieutenant topped my list. It became the benchmark of what I knew I could achieve if I worked hard and fully committed myself to it.

Your achievements might consist of earning a scholarship, graduating with honors, being named All-State or All-American in sports, community service awards, letters of commendation, etc. Display copies of your certificates and documents in your manual with the same pride as you would display them on your wall.

In the goals section of your manual, you should insert

pictures of those things you want to acquire or achieve. They can be career goals such as becoming a regional manager or VP within five years, or it could be owning a home at the beach or lakeshore.

My manual is filled with pictures of beautiful places I want to visit and automobiles I'd love to own. Many of these goals I have achieved, and I've inserted photos in my manual to chronicle those events. If you love beautiful clothes, then put pictures of fashions in your manual. If there's a particular type of boat, sports car, or classic car you desire, then showcase pictures of these dreams in your manual. As I said, your manual is a living scrapbook that should be constantly reviewed and updated. Your pictures serve as visual stimulation to keep you inspired and working toward that goal.

I've also printed out motivational and inspirational quotes from books I've read and pasted these into my manual. In fact, I've even generated some slogans of my own, such as "Keep your eyes on the prize."

Fundamentals of Selling

For me, periodically reviewing my inspiration manual is like having one of those energy boosting drinks. It rejuvenates my spirits and stimulates me to press on even harder. Believe me when I tell you that putting together your own inspiration manual will definitely prove to be a worthwhile endeavor that can continue to inspire you throughout your sales career. I urge you to get started on this worthwhile project right away.

You're going to discover that some days you'll need to kick-start your enthusiasm. It happens to us all. You'd rather sleep an extra hour or just lounge on the sofa watching *Headline News* or the *Today Show*. It's so easy to just remain in that nonthreatening comfort zone and not have to risk rejection than to go out and get after it. You reconcile yourself by doing some busywork like checking e-mail or doing an expense report. Sound familiar? But, such indulgences can definitely cost you in terms of your sales performance.

So how can you overcome these hurdles? Just give yourself a motivational boost by reviewing your inspiration

Staying on Track

manual and eyeballing that 28 foot Sea Ray boat you dream of owning. Or, you can play back a mental tape of a successful morning you recently had where everything clicked because you got up early and took a nice walk to get your mind right. You may have listened to a motivational tape during your walk. Then you were on the phone or en route to your first appointment by 7:30 or 8:00.

You'll find that it's amazing how quickly the positive energy will start to flow when you just push yourself over that first hurdle. The lesson you should take away from this chapter on Staying on Track is that it requires constant effort on your part to maintain your momentum. It doesn't perpetuate itself. You must be the primary driver of your own destiny. Go for it!

Best wishes for success and satisfaction

in all your selling endeavors.

Jim Norred

Epilogue

– Onward the Quest!

I once asked a Yellow Pages artist friend of mine to draw me a picture of a Don Quixote looking character holding up a shield with the words "Onward the Quest" on it. I still have this picture hanging in my office. It symbolized my quest for those things that were important in my life. Success is not a destination but rather a journey. Your quest for excellence must be ongoing. It is forged through a belief in yourself and a strong desire to be a winner. How do you accomplish this? By developing your ability to meet and overcome adversity and the everyday challenges of life. Here are some of my recommendations for achieving that goal.

- Read regularly, not just for entertainment but for enrichment.

- Recognize that you don't necessarily have to be the best at what you do, but you should certainly strive to be among the best.

- Always keep integrity the cornerstone of your work ethic. Honesty is an asset that no one can take away from you unless you allow them to.

- Always take pride in the professionalism of your performance.

- If your fundamental selling skills remain sound, then finesse and personal flair will gradually follow.

- Commit now to begin developing your inspiration manual. Refer to it regularly and update it often.

- Be all that you can be!

Jim Norred

Sales Call Evaluation

Date: _____

Sales Rep: _____

Prospect: _____

Address: _____

City: _____

State: _____ Zip: _____

Phone: _____

E-mail: _____

(1) Describe your approach statement or opening question.

(2) How effective do you feel it was?

(3) What sales visual aids were used, and in hindsight, perhaps should have been used?

(4) How could your approach have been improved?

(5) What were the primary objections or obstacles?

(6) How did you respond to them?

(7) How effective was your response?

(8) Describe your closing attempts.

(9) Which one succeeded or failed?

(10) What might have worked better?

(11) If not sold or closed, what is your follow-up strategy?

(12) What do you feel would be the prospect's most likely reason to buy?

SalesCadre.com

Go For It!

Index

A

"Action" close, 123-125
Aerobics, mental, 12
"Alternate of Choice" close, 129
Amway, 3
Analyze-Strategize-Crystallize concept, 62, 73-74
Annuities, 35
Approach question, 32
Approach, sales, 19-37, 44
Arouse curiosity, 26, 48
Arouse curiosity maneuver, 37
"Attention" phase, 19

B

Backdoor approach, 141
Back-up supplier strategy, 42, 109
"Ben Franklin Balance Sheet" close, 136-137
"Benefit" (defined), 72
Best Sales comeback, 39-41, 104

"Blitzing" objections, 105-109
"Bracketing" question, 63
"Bridging", 97, 178
Buffett, Jimmy, 181
Buyer fears, 166
Buyer's remorse, 80, 93
Buying Motives, 57, 70, 88-89

C

Call Back strategy, 140-141, 148
Cataloging countermeasures, 165-166
Cheerleading squad, 150
Closed ended question, 62-63
Closing, 119-144
Cold calling, 155-158
Complacency, 22
"Concession" close, 130-131
Consultative selling, 122, 148-151, 159, 171-174
Conviction step, 80-82, 85-88
Covey, Stephen R., 16, 64, 96, 160, 182

Creative thinking, 31-33, 36-37, 169
"Criteria" close, 134-135
Customer (defined), 12
Cyberpower, 151

D

Datsun 300ZX, 85-86
Dead end question, 60-61
Deregulation – telephone industry, 31-34
Design/performance spec's 172-173
Diagnosing, 14, 43, 55-64, 122, 139
Diagnosing openers, 61
Dialogue starters, 61
"Direct" close, 128, 137, 170
Disarming techniques, 111-117
Don Quixote, 189
Drop back maneuver, 21

E

Empathy, 97
Exhilaration, 6

F

Facebook, 182
"Facilitate" (defined), 80, 133
"Feature" (defined), 72
Feature & Benefit list, 22
Feature/Benefit formula, 73
Federal Trade Commission, 47, 93-94, 158

"Feel, Felt, Found" formula, 21, 97, 104

G

"Gatekeeper" (defined), 51-52, 157
General Telephone Directory Company, 199

H

Hesitancy - buyer, 169-171
Hostile buyer, 15, 27, 111-117, 160
Hostile encounters, 111-117, 160
Hoovers.com, 47

I

I'm just looking defense, 27-28, 87
I'm not interested, 20-21, 25, 33, 44, 95, 106
Indifferent buyer, 14
Inspiration manual, 183-187
Interconnect telephone company, 31
Interest creating remark, 25
iPhone™, 102, 151
Isolate step, 99-101

L

Last minute salvage strategy, 175
Long term care insurance, 76-77
Low-probability prospects, 166

M

Macaulay, Thomas B. (quote), 68, 119
McDonald's restaurant, 2-3
MCI long distance, 34
"Mind Opening" question, 153
"Minor Point" close, 125, 128, 170
MP3, 70
Multi-level marketing organizations, 3
Multiple bids strategy, 174-175

N

No perceived need, 76-77
Not interested, 20-21, 25, 33, 44, 95, 106

O

Objections (defined), 95
Objections handling formula, 96-103
Open ended question, 62
Opening question, 58-60
Opening remark – see Opening statement
Opening statement, 19-21, 26, 34-35, 153
Opening statement formula, 21
"Opportunity" calls, 155-158
Opportunity on-ramp question, 60-61

P

Perceived need, 69-70, 76-77
Peripheral problem strategy, 26, 30, 50, 148, 174
Pre-call, 167-168
Pre-call psyche up ritual, 150
Predominant buying motives, 57, 70, 88-89
Preemptive questions, 139-140
Preliminary pleasantries, 176-179
Price objection analogy, 100, 161, 176
Probing question, 60
Product knowledge, 28, 68
"Professional" (defined), 1
Prospect (defined), 12
Prospecting, 155-158

Q

Qualifying prospects, 56

R

Request for Quotes (RFQ's), 172
"Return Serve" close, 129-130
Roosevelt, Teddy (quote), 28

S

Sales approach, 19-37, 44
Sales Cadre (defined), 5
Sales Call Evaluation form, 71, 155, 191-193
Sales Track board game, 17
Sales Track graphic, 7

Sales visual, 69-70, 102, 140, 154, 158
"Schlock" artist (defined), 79
Secretarial barrier, 51-52, 157
"Sell me this pen" interview tactic, xvi-xviii
Selling (defined), 10
SellingPower.com, 46
"Sharp Angle" close, 129-130
Smoke screens, 104
"So What?" tactic, 76
Spark interest maneuver, 37, 48
Sprint long distance, 34
Stalls, 95-96, 103-104, 110, 133, 139
Staples "Easy" button, 164
Stephen Covey (Dr.), 16, 64, 96, 160, 182
"Stun" Statement, 39-41, 104
Suppliers checklist, 42
"Subordinate Point" close, 125
"Sympathetic" buyer, 14

T

Tacit approval, 120-123
Teaser button, 33, 163-164
Teddy Roosevelt (quote), 28
Telephone approach, 46-49
Testimonial letters, 102, 141, 148
"Think it over" strategy, 133-137
"Tie Downs" (defined), 82-83
Trade shows, 151-153
Transactional selling, 148
"Trial" close, 102, 128-129

V

"Validation" articles, 26, 32, 141, 148, 154, 159
Validation selling, 159
Vendor Qualifications checklist, 140
Visual aids, 22, 32, 34-35, 42, 69-70, 102, 154, 158
Visualization selling, 85-88
Voicemail tactics, 47-48

W

When to close, 11, 102, 110, 119-120, 128.

Y

YouTube videos, 151

Z

Zig Ziglar (quote), xii

About the Author

Jim Norred started his sales career in 1973 selling Yellow Pages advertising for General Telephone Directory Company in Florida. After only a year and a half, Jim was promoted to regional sales trainer due to an excellent sales record, his intense customer focus, and Jim's superb attention to detail. In this role, Jim had responsibility for administering classroom as well as field training for new Yellow Pages sales representatives. Within fourteen months, Jim was promoted once again to district sales manager. In 1977, Jim was recruited by a competitor of General Telephone Directory Company to develop and administer their corporate sales training program. This focus on designing and delivering excellence in sales training for companies continued throughout the remainder of Jim's active corporate career. Jim has over 35 years experience in sales training and development and continues in this regard as an independent business consultant. Jim's training style has been described as "easy to follow and comprehend". He has developed sales training programs and manuals for the Yellow Pages industry, interconnect telephone companies, electric utilities, and the safety apparel industry. Across such diverse industries, Jim's sales training message remains fundamentally the same. "Selling is knowing what to say, how to say it, and when to say it."